Jesus at Work among the
Next Generation of the Church

**Rod White**

Outskirts Press, Inc.
Denver, Colorado

The opinions expressed in this manuscript are solely the opinions of the author and do not represent the opinions or thoughts of the publisher. The author has represented and warranted full ownership and/or legal right to publish all the materials in this book.

A Circle of Hope
Jesus at Work among the Next Generation of the Church
All Rights Reserved.
Copyright © 2009 Rod White
v4.0

Cover Photo © 2009 Rod White.

This book may not be reproduced, transmitted, or stored in whole or in part by any means, including graphic, electronic, or mechanical without the express written consent of the publisher except in the case of brief quotations embodied in critical articles and reviews.

Outskirts Press, Inc.
http://www.outskirtspress.com

ISBN: 978-1-4327-4420-5

Outskirts Press and the "OP" logo are trademarks belonging to Outskirts Press, Inc.

PRINTED IN THE UNITED STATES OF AMERICA

# Welcome to the Book!

*A Circle of Hope,* the book, is a bit like a salad, which is a bit like the church called Circle of Hope in the Philadelphia region — lots of flavors all mixed up and tasty. Enjoy!

1) It is based on the "proverbs" of Circle of Hope; so sometimes, it may read a bit like the book of Proverbs in the Bible — a somewhat **random collection**. You won't find too much systematic theology here.
2) It follows parts of the story of how Circle of Hope, the people, developed over the past decade or so; so sometimes it has the flavor of a **memoir**. You'll find all sorts of references about what's been going on for the past decade, in real time and virtually!
3) It is all about trying to put into practice what Jesus is teaching in the here and now; so most of the time it reads like **theology done in community**, because that is how the book got written. Thanks to the seminarians and all the others who got it going, thanks to everyone who commented online and improved it, and thanks to everyone who is yet to join in the dialogue. We all have something to contribute to what God is doing next (see chapter 4!).

There is no way to write about the Church, much less Circle of Hope, as if the Church is a concept, or a past historical fact, or an image trapped in time — or anything else that usually appears in a book. The church is an organism or it is dead (see chapter 8!). So keep in mind that whatever is in this book is part of a developing story. We're telling the story, but, as you can tell, we doubt that the last chapter has even begun! Let's write it together.

We'll trust you with all that.

# Contents

Chapter 1: The Safe Place......................................................1
   *Jesus Story: Jesus and the woman caught in adultery, John 8*

Chapter 2: The Next Generation of the Church........................13
   *The Story: Jesus and Paul, the fools, 1 Corinthians 4:10*

Chapter 3: Revealing Jesus Incarnationally ..............................25
   *The Story: Jesus the Incarnation, John 20*

Chapter 4: Moving with What the Spirit is Doing Next .............39
   *The Story: Jesus and Philip the pioneers, Acts 8*

Chapter 5: Going Deep with God ...........................................53
   *The Story: Jesus walks on water, Matthew 13 and 14*

Chapter 6: Doing the Word....................................................67
   *The Story: Jesus at Matthew's, Matthew 9*

Chapter 7: Generating Justice and Hope in
Our Neighborhood .................................................................79
   *The Story: Jesus tells the story of the merciful Samaritan,*
   *Luke 10*

Chapter 8: Building Community as a Living Organism..............95
   *The Story: Jesus and the Sons of Thunder, Matthew 20*

Chapter 9: Maintaining the Dialogue.....................................109
   *The Story: Jesus tells the story of the two sons. Luke 15*

Chapter 10: Fomenting Diversity and Reconciliation ...............125
   *The Story: Jesus and the women —*
   *in Lebanon and Samaria, Mark 7 and John 4*

Chapter 11: Expressing Our New Selves ................................137
   *The Story: Jesus and Nicodemus, John 3*

Chapter 12: Leading as a Team.............................................151
   *The Story: Jesus prays for us, John 17*

Chapter 13: Sharing Resources .............................................165
   *The Story: Jesus and the Seventy, Luke 10*

CHAPTER 1

# The Safe Place
*Jesus Story: Jesus and the woman caught in adultery, John 8*

One day long ago, my ancient pickup made it fifty miles from home! Great! But then it began to rain. The truck didn't run so well in the rain. So I ended up pushing it, alone…somewhere. People in very nice cars splashed by. But a Spanish-mainly gardener, in a smoking station wagon filled with tools, pulled alongside and held up jumper cables, "Si?" Thank God for the people who make a safe place!

Much later in life, but not too long ago, I was wandering around Philadelphia looking for partners in my mission to build a part of the Church God wants to build. I got lost a lot. But I soon found out that there are a lot of loving black ladies who monitor the streets of my city! It was usually fruitless to try to stop nicely dressed men in suits to get advice (a terrible generalization, but that's my experience). But one lady not only stopped to listen, she walked with me several blocks to make sure I got where I needed to go! She made Philly a safe place for me. There can't be too many people like that.

I want to be part of a church like those people — a people who are a safe place. Circle of Hope may not have always *been* that church for the past decade, but we never stop longing to become one. Rather than building another one of those unsafe places we never wanted to inhabit again, we said, "We will be *a circle of hope in Jesus Christ, a safe place to explore and express God's* love." I hope, this first chapter feels a little bit like that — like you were wandering around with a dead battery and someone loved you just the way you are, or you were lost and someone directed you where you needed to go. This chapter is meant to be a safe place for liberals and conservatives, Batman, adulteresses, post-Christian Europeans, heroic generals, and, of course, you — just the kind of place Jesus always builds.

## I hope we're reacting to the right things

If we seem a little reactionary as you are getting to know us, that's a little true, though not our favorite attribute. We want to *be* something, not just *not* something. But we can't hide all the stray bits of reactivity in us. Just saying "we are a safe place" implies that some churches just aren't! But some churches aren't. People have been dominated, abused, bamboozled, threatened and diminished in church for ages. What's more, Christianity has been such an *"ity"* for so long it has quantified and squashed people into whatever the latest spiritual*"ity"* is, over and over! That's worth reacting to! — and I think it is one reason God invented Circle of Hope. He needs another outpost of his counter rebellion against all the coercion going on in the name of Jesus.

Like the recent revival of the old musical, South Pacific, on Broadway is bringing up, "You have to be carefully taught" to coerce people rather than provide a safe place for them to recover from their sin addiction. One woman read this chapter and wrote: "I can listen to my non-christian friends tell me all sorts of things that I do not morally agree with, I never hold them to some higher law or condemn them for what they may have done wrong. It is my fellow brothers and sisters in Christ that I can not stand when they continue to live in sin. I silently condemn them even though I have plenty of sins that I commit everyday." She was taught. Why *wouldn't* you condemn the Christians if what you learned in the church meetings was all about being condemned and condemning others in order to keep it all perfect lest someone find out the Christians aren't perfect, which would make Jesus look bad, and then people wouldn't choose to believe in Him, and then the whole church would be unsuccessful, its market share would be absorbed by a jumbotron preacher, and it would be your fault?

I don't think God is into coercion. He doesn't even coerce us into following him. And I don't think he's on the side of people who have the power to force their delusions on others — and who actually go ahead and do it! Much to the contrary, God on the cross in Jesus Christ is the ultimate rebellion against the godless powers that dominate the world. The cross, among all the other things it means, is a call to arms against powers that rope people into joining in all the ways that destroy humans and despoil the planet we have been given.

Coercion is the powerful controlling the weak, the manipulative steering the gullible or the audacious herding the unsuspecting. It is a technique many religious people have mastered — sometimes they do it unwittingly because it's all they know, but sometimes it is hard to believe they don't know exactly what they are doing. As soon as you're in the meeting, they are insisting you are wrong and suggesting you are stupid. They are going to save you and straighten you up — implying, of course, that *they* are not wrong or stupid. One *has* to rebel against that, right? I do — at least I have to admit I am no good at submitting myself to self-proclaimed authorities or even authorities that are too self-proclaiming.

When it comes to a big part of the Church I know, I feel like that poor general in Iraq, sometime in 2005, who was reacting to Vice President Dick Cheney. The Vice President said, "I think they're in the last throes, if you will, of the insurgency", insinuating that the insurgents were on their last legs. The general felt compelled to say, "That's not so." He spoke out against the man who had enough power to sell the country on a dubious cause and to fuel it with young lives and billions of dollars — the very man who had repeatedly used his big bully pulpit to shame anyone who pointed out his transgressions against the truth by insisting his detractors were speaking out against freedom and undermining the honor of every self-sacrificing soldier! It is frightening to heed a call to rebel against power like that! But, I shudder to say, I am with the general. Unbridled power, enforced delusions, deception that results in dead children, all cause me to say, "No!"

I have to keep practicing saying "No!" when I need to, or I get coerced into all sorts of sinful things. When I was first a Christian, my mentor in ministry shouted and shamed and threatened us from his raised-up pulpit every Sunday. When I went to my weekly intern meeting on Tuesday, I tended to shout back. The secretaries loved it. But my overseers identified that rebellion as my sin. So be it.

Not long ago someone was smoking outside our door on Broad St. after the PM (Public Meeting). I overheard someone saying under their breath with disgust as they were leaving (maybe for my benefit, they thought), "Don't be smoking in front of church; take your cigarette down the street." I wanted to light up in rebellion (even though I think death-defying smoking is kind of dumb).

Long ago one of our covenant members decided he was gay and left his family. A young couple in the church was appalled that we did not kick him to the street in some kind of message-sending way. They questioned the church's holiness. I told them it would be good if they took their coercive judgment and lack of love elsewhere (even though I thought parts of their "opinion" made some sense).

That's what I have become. I can't take it: Christians protecting their turf — using their power to kick people who are wrong or wronged, who are weak, foolish, or threatening — teaching by means of fear and judgment, telling people, "You'll go to hell if you don't agree with me," — dividing up the church with endless arguing — leading people by playing upon their broken sense of self and their endless capacity for guilt — I think that is all wrong. It dishonors God, who went to the cross with an invitation to everyone to be saved, who died for us while we were sinners, who knew us, loved us and accepted us as soon as we were born, and who is doing whatever is possible to make sure we can be born anew, who saved us, purposely not coercing us in the process.

## The safe place we are and aren't

Attempting to work all that conviction into the character of our safe place is hardly simple. It is easier to *not* be something than to *be* something. There are many problems with trying to be a church that is a safe place. One of the biggest is that being saved may not be the same as feeling safe. Many people feel *God* is very coercive, which is one reason they feel justified in avoiding him or out-and-out rebelling against him. After all, Jonathan Edwards (1703-58) branded the U.S. imagination with the picture of an angry God dangling us sinners like a spider over a fire until we submitted fully to his domination! It has become a cliché that nuns think a good rap on the knuckles is a good way to cultivate good Catholics. I don't think Jesus really wants to save people that way.

God can use most of what he is given to advance his purposes, but it's too bad he has to overcome so much bogus stuff done in his name in order to reveal his character and get in touch with us! God is not Zeus firing thunderbolts from heaven and capriciously doing whatever weird thing he wants to do to prove he's in charge. God is not Shiva whose terror gets poured into an idol to placate. God is the Father of our Lord Jesus Christ, who made himself less than a servant, freeing us when we didn't know we were locked up, loving us before we loved back, giving us life before we knew how to receive it, wooing us personally back into a growing mutual relationship. God in Jesus is the savior, who keeps us from dying under the weight of our sin and leads us out of the ruin of our self-destruction. Jesus is that safe place: *"I have come into the world as a light, so that no one who believes in me should stay in darkness. "As for the person who hears my words but does not keep them, I do not judge him. For I did not come to judge the world, but to save it."* (John 12:46-7)

That is the God we follow. The next church is a circle of hope in Jesus Christ, called to be a safe place to explore and express God's love. We want to develop a collection of love-behaviors that match God's commitment to us: accept people where they are right now — hope for the best for everyone — stick with people on their journey — protect everyone's road from danger — give people places to be nurtured — help everyone get what they need.

That's the kind of people we have always wanted to be, and I think it is who we have become. But we'll have to keep working at it — it's not like it is a normal way to be. If you were listening to these thoughts in the relative safety of our meeting room, I would ask you to turn to someone and, "Tell them just how safe you *really* feel in the room right now." I suspect a lot of people would be dealing with all the things that make us nervous or frightened when we are together. Something is usually making each of us feel unsafe no matter where we are — in the bosom of God's family or not! We need to keep acknowledging those things. Because, chances are, no matter how many times we reassure someone that we are a safe place, we will not make them feel safe every moment according to their personal standards of safety. Nobody can really do that.

What's more, there are a few things many of us wish were safe to be and do that we won't try to arrange, even if you ask us! For instance:

- We are not on the side of people who kill and dominate others by economic, military or social means in order to keep themselves wealthy and safe-feeling behind the walls of power. I don't believe that keeping other people down or keeping them behind big walls, like our government tries to do, really keeps anyone safe, anyway. Like Mary exulted: *"He has brought down rulers from their thrones but has lifted up the humble."* (Luke 1:52) If you want to pursue a delusional safety, we can't help you.
- We are not a safe place away from Jesus. We carry a revelation; we did not make it up. We can't adjust the reality that Jesus is Lord, or deny the fact that we trust Him, in order to make someone feel better. If you want to be safe from Jesus we can't help you.
- We are not a safe place to avoid transformation. The presence of God's Holy Spirit creates an inevitable pull toward spiritual growth and wholeness. We are going with it, not fighting it. If you try to lead us elsewhere, we won't follow you.

## Aspiring to live like Jesus, the safe place

We are trying to be like Jesus in John 8. Jesus, in himself, is the safe place, and we, as his body, aspire to be like him. We want our story to be like this account of his life:

At one point Jesus went to Jerusalem and made his presence known in the Temple. He *"went to the Mount of Olives. At dawn he appeared again in the temple courts, where all the people gathered around him, and he sat down to teach them. The teachers of the law and the Pharisees brought in a woman caught in adultery."*

A group of powerful men who had the authority to coerce and had the audacity to exercise their power sought Jesus out. No one knows whether they dragged this woman out of her bed or not, and no one knows where the *man* caught in adultery was. But we can imagine a group of men fighting for what they believe in. Imagine Bill O'Reilly vs. Mahmoud Ahmadinejad (you might need to keep Google handy at times, while you're reading this!).

Similar people often fight for their convictions in the Church. Encountering such conflict is like an occupational hazard for Christians. I have had numerous afraid or appalled people contact me over the years, as their pastor, very concerned about someone caught red-handed in sin, just like the adulterous woman dragged before Jesus. Sexual sin seems to be the scariest or most appalling to people — but I've heard tales of the sin of using styrofoam cups, the sin of buying a too-expensive car, the sin of letting greed decide where a family will move, the sin of abusing women, the sin of being an unconnectable slacker — all sorts of other things, too. Concerned people catch people red-handed, bring the person forward, usually in absentia, and say, "What will the church do?" Somehow, we think we will be safe when justice is served. These lawyers and religious leaders who came to Jesus probably thought that, too.

*"They made [the woman] stand before the group and said to Jesus, "Teacher, this woman was caught in the act of adultery. In the Law, Moses commanded us to stone such women. Now what do you say?" They were using this question as a trap, in order to have a*

*basis for accusing him."*

They wanted Jesus to answer the age-old question: "What will happen if the rule is not followed?" The standard fear of coercive people is that, "Everyone will just go hog wild; that's what will happen if anyone is allowed to get away with something." Or at least God will look bad because God doesn't keep his rules. These men knew that the Law of Moses says to stone adulterers — although it had been a long time since anyone did that. They wanted to test Jesus, like people often want to test us: "Will you follow the Bible? Do you have any spiritual fire, or are you just a flaky bunch of do-gooders who are soft on crime — a bunch of liberals?" The men probably already thought Jesus was a liberal. They thought he was just making things up as he was going along and not toeing the line like they did. So they concocted a situation to point that out.

Men like that made me the rebel I am today. Jesus has a lot cooler head about the whole thing than I do. I desperately need to respond to people like Jesus does, but I often get mad. I heard that a daughter of some former friends of mine had sex with her not-so-reputable boyfriend and ended up getting pregnant. These devoted church people organized a special time for their daughter to get up in front of the church and apologize for her sin. Out of their own shame, they brought her before the "authorities" for her "stoning." She's still wearing her "scarlet letter" around town, and so is her baby.

*Jesus bent down and started to write on the ground with his finger. When they kept on questioning him, he straightened up and said to them, "If any one of you is without sin, let him be the first to throw a stone at her." Again he stooped down and wrote on the ground.*

That's one of the best answers in the Bible, isn't it? I wish the church had done that in response to my friends' daughter.

*At this, those who heard began to go away one at a time, the older ones first, until only Jesus was left, with the woman still standing there. Jesus straightened up and asked her, "Woman, where are they? Has no one condemned you?"*

*"No one, sir," she said.*

*"Then neither do I condemn you,"* Jesus declared. *"Go now and leave your life of sin."*

Here is where Jesus demonstrates the essence of what it means to be a safe place. He said, "Then neither do I condemn."

- The woman is condemnable. "I do not condemn you," Jesus says.
- She is a disgrace, a shame to the town, and an affront to God. "I did not come to condemn but to save," Jesus says.
- The law says she deserved death. "The law proves her condemnable. But I do not condemn her."
- She is humiliated, weak, no doubt ashamed, scared, wondering how she ever ended up in the dirt like this with Jesus. Jesus looks at her and says, "I do not condemn you."

That's the kind of people we are trying to be in a world where no one seems to think Christians would ever be like that — not even the Christians!

## Something more needs to happen

You know that Jesus said something else, too. Just not condemning someone is not all there is to being a safe place. There is more.

First, he said to those men who had taken up stones and were ready to kill this exposed woman at his command, *"Go and leave your life of sin."* I don't think he just said that to the woman. I think he said it to everyone. When he told the men, *"You who are without sin cast the first stone,"* he told those hypocrites who put themselves in the place of God and condemned someone before their time to, *"Go and leave your life of sin."* Jesus asserted his own authority over the situation — "I will take care of judgment. You go ponder why you would dare to take my place when you deserve her place."

Then he said to the one who was sure she would get what she deserved, *"Go and leave your life of sin."* — Respond to this grace I have won for you this day.

That's the whole picture of being safe. Jesus frees us from condemnation so we are free to *live* freed of condemnation. That's

## A CIRCLE OF HOPE

what Circle of Hope, the safe place, is for, too — living.

But living requires more than freedom, and it does not come automatically to any of us. It would be nice if everyone holding rocks dropped their rocks and said, "OK. I get it," as soon as Jesus was revealed. Likewise, it would be nice if Jesus spoke to sinners and they always got up out of the dirt and said, "No problem. I'll leave my life of sin." Once in a while people turn right around and follow. But more often than not, our safe place is sticky with the sexual issues that mean so much to us and is sticky with all sorts of other imponderable circumstances, as well. Like Jesus, I want people, myself included, to leave their life of sin. So no matter how we meet up with someone, we start from Where we meet them and stay with them until they get a chance to get out of whatever brokenness they need to get out of. We don't overlook their sin; we bring hope to it. I think that is as safe as it gets, this side of the new heaven and earth that's coming.

Thank God Batman knows all about that, too, and put it out there on the screen for us to ponder the time before last! The whole movie (if you even *remember* 2005) was about Batman's choice whether to give his life to provide a safe place like Jesus, or not — at least that's the way I look at it. In *Batman Begins*, it is not a foregone conclusion as to which way the caped crusader is going to go — good or bad. We find out that he was originally recruited to join up with the forces that want to destroy Gotham City for its sin. But he also had another choice. He was also pulled to be like his murdered father, to be compassionate and to help save Gotham somehow. Ultimately he decides to sacrifice his life to make Gotham a safe place for people to be transformed. At the end of the movie, when Batman has defeated the forces of destruction, Lieutenant Gordon says, "I never told you thank you." Batman peers back at him out of his cowl and says, "And you will never have to," and flies off the roof.

Let's be like that incarnation of Batman! A good person creates the safe place where people can be saved. It would be nice to thank them, but they'd do it anyway because that is just what they do!

## It is a new era

We who follow Jesus know that love like Batman's (at least that one) is elemental to this final leg of God's redemption project. Even if people get a little crazy and start shouting, "You're soft on sin! You need to take a stand and get coercive! You are letting people get away with stuff! We caught her red handed!" — I want to give *them* a safe place to explore and express God's love, too.

It is a new era. A lot of the Christianity of the past 100 years in this country has been very powerful: hard sermons threatening hell — harsh priests and nuns promising punishment if you don't follow the rules — lots of relentless fighting about logic and rejecting of friends and relatives who stay on the other side of an argument. People have gotten so burned by all that coercion it has helped move Europe and North America towards the post-Christian column.

We can do better. We may not always *be* it, but we sure *want* to be part of a people who are relating the Jesus-down-in-the-dirt way, the ever-surprising way by which people find out that they are not as condemned as they feel or deserve. I hope we keep finding joy in looking into a hurting, angry, hopeless, mean-spirited, depressed, or violent person's face with love and keep finding joy in winning the right to tell them, "Go and leave your life of sin. With God's help, I'll do whatever I can to make that possible."

CHAPTER **2**

# The Next Generation of the Church
*The Story: Jesus and Paul, the fools, 1 Corinthians 4:10*

In 1995, a few of us were sitting around in my newly-settled living room in West Philly considering what we would call the new church that was gestating. It was just like my family sitting around the dinner table not long ago suggesting names for the first member of the next generation of the White family kicking around inside my daughter-in-law. Something was growing and we needed to say what it is.

Admittedly, as far as the church goes, in the back of the few minds gathered, a search was going on for a cool na me. And it is very hard to find a cool name for a church! Every name that sounds cool sounds like you are trying to be cool. What's more, we were kind of afraid we might attract people who are attracted to cool names. So we settled for searching for a name that honestly described what we wanted to be. We came up with Circle of Hope.

If you think that is a cool name, thanks. Regardless, within that name are a couple of things we think God is giving to a needy generation.

1) *The Circle*. It's like sitting around the campfire, or around a table in a bar booth, or maybe like covered wagons getting attacked. However it manifests itself, the circle is all about being a place for community to grow, about being face-to-face in basic circles of ten, about being knit together in a network of congregations that

overcome divisions and share resources. Plus, it is all about being something that can roll somewhere further — and very possibly rock. We didn't predict that people would just call us "Circle," but that is what happened in a lot of places.

2) *Hope.* We thought "hope" was probably going to sound cheesy, since it had an utter lack of irony. But that's what we have to offer to people who are often, underneath their perfect or purposely-not-perfect facade, pretty hopeless — about themselves, about the world, and about the possibility of knowing God. I suppose it is a belligerent kind of naiveté we have held on to in the spirit of these lines from Paul's letter to the Romans:

*We have peace with God through our Lord Jesus Christ, through whom we have gained access by faith into this grace in which we now stand. And we rejoice in the hope of the glory of God. ...And hope does not disappoint us, because God has poured out his love into our hearts by the Holy Spirit, whom he has given us. (Romans 5:1-5).*

We're daring to be "fools," in the eyes of many, like the Apostle Paul, who wrote to the big-city Christians in Rome about his hope. The story of his relationship with Christ is a good model for us. He had to admit that what he was doing didn't make much sense to a lot of people, but he had to do it.

Peace, standing in grace, joy, suffering with a vision, facing down disappointment, love, the Holy Spirit — that's what we live for, too — or at least what we *want* to live for. We think we should just put it out there before anyone gets the wrong idea. Not that we expect a lot of people to get much of an idea about us at all, really, since we're easy to ignore, and not that we expect every Jesus-follower to feel all excited about putting anything out there, since Christians are about as good as anyone at pretending that they aren't needy — but putting it out there it is what we do.

## The Mission

If the love of God were just sitting in our hearts, it would not be the love of God. A circle of hope inevitably expresses that love. We have a mission to see what love — created, fueled, and motivated by God's love — can do to redeem the world.

Yes, we want to keep using the word "mission," and not just in honor of *Mission Impossible*, which is how our mission often feels. We want to keep using the word even though we are not too fond of being connected with the unattractive stereotypes of "missionaries" putting top hats on Hawaiians or showing up with name tags on your door step. But we can't think of a better word to describe what we do.

The word is not the only problem. Just the idea that we might have a mission often makes people question us about our grandiosity or audacity. What do *you* think when we say our "mission" or our "purpose" or "the reason Circle of Hope needs to not sell out to Rupert Murdoch" is: *We build the church for the next generation by the power of the Holy Spirit?*

Some people think that is radical. Maybe it is. But it is not hard to understand. We are providing an opportunity for the people who are growing up next to meet God and be one with his people. We are especially concerned with those 18-35 year olds who are still not hard of heart and mind, since they are notoriously left out of the Church.

This mission is not a new idea, of course: *Since my youth, O God, you have taught me, and to this day I declare your marvelous deeds. Even when I am old and gray, do not forsake me, O God, till I declare your power to the next generation , your might to all who are to come.* (Psalm 71:17-18)

The psalmist is sounding kind of tribal there, isn't he? We can go with that. We feel an obligation to transmit lore, to tell the secrets of the spirit world and to initiate loved ones into reality. After more than a decade of working at it, a few of us are even getting old and gray, like in the Psalm, but by and large, we're not. It doesn't take age to be an agent of transformation. If you are 22, there must be a 17 year old who needs to hear you declare the power of God before they can't hear so well anymore.

Some of our more sociologically-minded friends aren't so sure about our persistent focus on an age group. They think older people are being left out. But they aren't really; we just call them into catering rather than being catered to. There is lots of place for them to come alongside and help us fulfill our calling. One reason God focused our attention on "the next generation" is obvious: the vast majority of people moving into our city are young. In Center City and Fishtown, where we have concentrated for years, you can't throw a rock out your door without hit the youth of America! But maybe even more, we know that this whole age group is *becoming* something, and everyone is gunning for them. They are not fully formed yet, even biologically. We are determined to give them a chance to meet Jesus before some other "missionary" wins them to the other "gospels" hunting them down with the most powerful communication devices the world has ever known.

The idea of being for the next generation has also come to mean that we are shooting for becoming the next generation of the church — the next model, the upgrade, the quantum leap into what everyone else thought might happen next, the appropriate adaptation to present realities. It is not that the old school was particularly bad — we're brazenly sampling it and appreciating all the genius God stored up when all those people were creating the church in *their* generation! We just want to go with God in the new school and keep going. We don't want to wake up in our agedness some day and realize we stopped listening and following about 1999 — even if 1999 was a great year!

OK. That was *some* explanation! Now let's get on with talking about meeting and loving real people with Jesus walking alongside us doing what Jesus does. Big ideas about mission don't make much sense unless someone does something to care about people, do they?

## Being Real

During the short lifetime of Circle of Hope, another phenomenon appeared on the scene: reality TV. *Survivor* on CBS is probably the show most people remember as one of the first examples, first airing in 2000. I got into it. But what really got me going was *The Real World San Francisco* with Puck and Pedro in 1994. And I am still in wonder over *I Want A Famous Face*, another MTV offering, first airing in 2004.

Viacom (owner of CBS and MTV) is still mining the hopes and dreams of the next generation to get an audience. In my mind there is a lot of similarity between what the networks have been trying to do and what Circle of Hope has been trying to do. Our missions have dissimilar ends, but they are certainly getting to know the same generation. See what you think.

There is a lot to be learned as the psychology and sociology of a generation is distilled into thirty minute episodes. And while this exploration might seem like a walk down memory lane at this point, it still helps us zero in on what a mission to the next generation or the next generation of the Lord's mission might be like. There is a very interesting generation of people being developed out there, and a lot of them show their stuff on reality TV.

1) **Apparently, an amazing number of the next generation want to be a star** (and the more cheap footage cable needs, the more chance they have to become one!). A few people have turned their brief reality show celebrity into a career, talent notwithstanding. Philadelphia has been well represented among these new celebs. Gervase Peterson, of Philadelphia and South Jersey, went from "Survivor 2000" to bits all over TV and on into parts in films. His career gives people a strange hope for making it in the strange world evolving before our eyes.

Circle of Hope can seem like a talent showcase, at times, too. One time a team put on springy antennae to lead worship! An amateur dancer did an interpretive dance to Madonna's "Frozen."

But we are more often a rehab for those who did not find their hopes realized in putting on a good show. Those who are not ready for prime time need a circle of hope. We're offering a very different opportunity — an end to the slavery of selling our perfect bodies or living up to a perfect image. We're going with Paul, the fool for Christ, who instructs us about what is real:

*For who makes you different from anyone else? What do you have that you did not receive? And if you did receive it, why do you boast as though you did not? Already you have all you want! Already you have become rich! You have become kings—and that without us! How I wish that you really had become kings so that we might be kings with you! For it seems to me that God has put us apostles on display at the end of the procession, like men condemned to die in the arena. We have been made a spectacle to the whole universe, to angels as well as to men. We are fools for Christ, but you are so wise in Christ! (1 Corinthians 4:7-10)*

Reality is received from God. If we are going to be stars, it should be as fools for Christ. We're getting lots of opportunity to make spectacles of ourselves in Philly.

**2) Apparently, there is an endless line up of relational train wrecks waiting to happen among the next generation.** The *Real World* has always been a celebration of "seven strangers, picked to live in a house and have their lives taped, and find out what happens when people stop being polite and start getting REAL." — Who will hook up? Who will break up? Who will be brought to despair? The dramatic possibilities are endless and the generation has a ready-made script inside waiting to be played out. *Real World Philadelphia* gave our city a moment of MTV glory in 2005. The show has just been renewed for 5 more years — there are more 19-22 years olds aching to play that part.

As a result, Circle of Hope has a lot of "drama" and that seems perfectly normal. We have people who head for the other congregation when they break up with their latest lover. We have become great at mediating the inevitable conflicts that come with living in proximity with strangers. But we are also a place where people can be introduced to the possibility of real community in Christ. Refugees from fractured relationships and families need a circle of hope. We're offering a different destiny than the broken families and vacuous hook ups many people are now used to. Paul's "foolish" approach guides us into how to be real:

*We are not trying to please men but God, who tests our hearts. You know we never used flattery, nor did we put on a mask to cover up greed—God is our witness. We were not looking for praise from men, not from you or anyone else. ...[W]e were gentle among you, like a mother caring for her little children. We loved you so much that we were delighted to share with you not only the gospel of God but our lives as well, because you had become so dear to us. (1 Thessalonians. 2:4-8)*

Reality is sharing God's love. We need God and his people to work through the drama of recovering from relational wounds. We are sharing with a lot of unexpectedly dear people in Philly.

**3) Apparently, people among the next generation will go to almost any length to be accepted or validated or just seem OK.** It can end up looking a little sad. The despair runs deep. The desperation to alleviate it can get scary. MTV's *I Want a Famous Face* had a short original run of despair in 2004. The episode no one seems to forget had to do with twin teen-age boys who wanted to change their acne-scarred, not-too-handsome, faces into Brad Pitt look-alikes through plastic surgery. They saved up for their extensive operations and viewers followed their progress before and after they went under the knife.

As a result, Circle of Hope is a gentle place for people facing real despair. So much of the church has been a platform for a diatribe to convince people they are sinful, flawed and in need of a Savior. Like I said last chapter, I think most people already know that and feel that deeply. Every image on the screen reminds a skinny/fat/less-than-marketable teen of every imperfection. Every week someone walks into the meeting hurting. The happy guy is a coke addict. The nice looking woman is anorexic. The missionary kid was abused. It would seem like an after-school program, if it were not happening! We're offering a real transformation into an image money can't buy. Again, even though the world acts like this is foolish, Paul insists our transformation in Christ leads to a reality that is our true destination:

*You have taken off your old self with its practices and have put on the new self, which is being renewed in knowledge in the image of its Creator. Here there is no Greek or Jew, circumcised or uncircumcised, barbarian, Scythian, slave or free, but Christ is all, and is in all. (Colossians 3:9-11)*

Reality crosses all barriers to gather us all into the kingdom of God. If we are ever going to feel OK in our own skins, we need to know ourselves in relation to Jesus. We are providing a place in Philly where people can face up to their God-given face.

We have good reasons for our corny name. People need a circle of hope to end up as a survivor living in the real world and facing up to their new selves in Christ. Like Paul, who wrote the antidotes to the poisonous reality TV above, we can seem a little foolish. We're getting used to the fact that our countercultural mission makes us fools for Christ, too.

## How to Build a Circle of Hope

Having a *mission* is not that easy to get used to, since when the word is used these days, it often seems like it shouldn't have been. Like I said, people think, at worst, of imperialist Euro-types being carried in sedan chairs by Africans, or at best they imagine Captain Pickard doing something out-of-this world. We're more grounded. Maybe we'd be better off to talk about our *purpose*, or *vocation*, or *raison d'etre* than our "mission." But we think people can eventually get a renewed meaning for the word.

Mostly, what we are talking about is building the church, expanding the kingdom, extending the acres of God's farm with newly-plowed fields. And we think we have been given a unique way to do it. Here's how we say it these days:

> *We build the church for the next generation*
> *by the power of the Holy Spirit*
> *- Multiplying cells that are authentic expressions of life in Christ*
> *- Forming congregations as diverse as the kingdom of God*
> *- Constructing a reconciling network to bring hope to the challenges of 21st century urban life.*

## We do it by multiplying cells that are authentic expressions of life in Christ

In an age in which machines and people are becoming one, in which overwhelming bureaucracies are sucking the life out of the last remaining wilderness areas, and in which huge corporations are enslaving people to debt and meaningless work, we want to build an organic community, an alternative society — just like Jesus has always been doing. The cell, a circle of ten people usually meeting in a home, is our basic building block.

I often wonder out loud about how God is staying in business with the competition he is getting in the postmodern West. The most prominent adaptations of the church are defending modernism and going down with that dinosaur, becoming totally adapted to the philosophies of capitalism, or throwing away thinking altogether and rushing headlong into some orgasmic experience. People are throwing away the church like an empty Skittles bag because it is so inauthentic. A cell is a weekly opportunity for authenticity. It is more than a game of *Survivor*, but it is similar. A cell is a small group of people thrown together in a somewhat hostile environment (the Philly metro!), but for a lot longer than 39 days (and no one is voted off the island!). It is our best example of how determined we are to encourage people to be themselves and go with whatever it is that God is going to create next — no agendas to follow or projects to complete, just loved ones having the struggle right out there in the open, needing to rely on each other to get to the end.

## We do it by forming congregations as diverse as the kingdom of God

In an age in which people are going "tribal" and splitting into atomized groups, clinging to some form of identity: sneaker brand, futbol team, professional association, ethnic enclave, sexual preference, Facebook network, etc., we still think there is a God-ordained unity that we can foment. We affirm everyone's tribe, but we hope they can relate in love. We long for our congregations to include everyone — receiving the benefits of being together and wearing the honor that comes from crossing the divisions that needlessly keep us at odds.

I often wonder how anyone can navigate the confusing array of church out there. It is so diverse and so not together. You've got the big dog on the block, the Catholic Church, still electing an aged pope to hold the line against whatever threatens tradition while others are having visions of Mary. You've got "fundamentalists" shouting obscenities at gay marchers and often fighting for the right to own automatic weapons. There are TV preachers promising prosperity, and an entire subculture devoted to purpose-driven everything. Most people I meet have simply turned it all off. Insert that turned-off attitude into the historically-divided-up town of Philly, where blacks, whites, Asians, rich and poor all seem to know the unspoken boundaries, and everything is horribly divided.

That's *our* Real World.

We just can't get it out of our heads that a congregation can welcome everyone — no matter what the evidence tells us otherwise. We do OK with age (although we look quite young — but even 20somethings and 30somethings don't hang that much, really). We do OK with status (although we are heavily educated and tend to be upwardly mobile — even if that means a bike messenger is moving up to electrician's helper), but we are less-successful with race. Our congregations are under 25% "minority," which is the ratio in the U.S., but Philly is 45% "black!" But we say, "Why not die trying?"

## We do it by constructing a reconciling network to bring hope to the challenges of 21st century urban life

The boiling pot of people that is the Northeast megalopolis from Washington, DC to Boston is a challenging place to live — 55 Million people with an economy that is bigger than the U.K or France. Our mega-region grew by about 20 million people from 1950-2000 and constitutes 17% of the U.S. population. What kind of people are we becoming and what kind of church flourishes and redeems here? Answering that question is our challenge.

I often wonder how anyone can rest long enough to consider what it means to live in such an environment! The new technology corridors like ours (and like from Hong Kong to Shenzhen or from Bangalore to Hyderabad) are creating a new kind of person living a next kind of life. The technology allows a faster pace filled with tons of info and demands a 24/7 response. We are being constantly reshaped. It is no wonder that gangly teen-agers assume they can be changed into Brad Pitt!

Circle of Hope is trying to bloom where we are planted. We're fulfilling one of the most ancient of obligations — transmitting the lore, telling the secrets of the Spirit world, initiating loved ones into reality. We're making disciples. The megalopolis strains to conform people to its ways and we keep working for justice and trying to tell the truth about what's going on with God. Through the course of being ourselves and telling our story, we're trying to impact the impacters. The best and brightest inhabit our megalopolis and they are inventing the philosophies and systems that will make the world what it is becoming. We want Jesus to get in there.

## Foolish Missionaries

I am always encouraged to keep going with my part of the mission when I read about how Paul, the fool, kept going with his part, along with the people in his circle. It is in the details of their struggle that I find hope for my own circle, planted, as it is, in what seems like hostile territory (see Acts 14 to start).

The mission is hard, but I love the reality of it. Without mission, I don't know how I can exercise my true self. That's how Paul could find leaders for the brand-new churches among people he barely knew! They wanted to be themselves! Our experience has been just as unlikely in Philly. Our partners in the cause have come from out of "nowhere."

They come into town from nowhere, live their lives in Christ, tell the story of Jesus, and people trust God again. It is amazing! In every generation, God does transformative things with people who trust him and trust others to him. In every era, against all odds, in an amazing variety of ways, God seems to find "fools" who will come up with more circles of hope.

CHAPTER 3

# Revealing Jesus Incarnationally
*The Story: Jesus the Incarnation, John 20*

This incident happened a long time ago and I *still* remember how guilty I felt. Two women came to the Public Meeting and we sang a song that really bothered them. It bothered them so much they made a point of telling a few of us that they would never come to another meeting because of it! It might be an odd song, but I don't think it is criminal! We wrote it for Psalm 77 using a Mozart violin concerto as the tune, but it ended up feeling like a soft, Texas two-step. (Well, that's just how it is).

The one line they really hated was: *"With my soul in tears, I call to you. When I feel my heart will drown, I look to you."* It put them over the edge.

"Why?" we asked.

They said, "We don't think Christians ought to be that whiney. We want to be more peppy." (That's what one of the women said). "We want Jesus to make us happy. You shouldn't be so messed up if you are a Christian."

Everyone else in the conversation with them looked at each other sheepishly, like maybe we were not living a triumphant-enough life and we needed to go get filled with the Spirit, rise above the problems of the earth and transcend our humanity like all those people on TV. I, for one, have been thinking about those young women ever since

and wondering if they, or we, really missed something. I think I told them then (but maybe not — it could just be in the mental replay I've been having ever since), but I would tell them now, if I got another chance, "My soul *is* in tears!" And it is because of _the following_":
*[Jesus] made himself nothing, taking the very nature of a servant, being made in human likeness. And being found in appearance as a man, he humbled himself and became obedient to death— even death on a cross! (Philippians 2:7- 8)*

Being obedient to death is not exactly "peppy," is it? What's more, "My heart *is* drowning!" I look to Jesus *when my heart is drowning* in the sea of humanity because of _the following_:
*I fill up in my flesh what is still lacking in regard to Christ's afflictions, for the sake of his body, which is the church. ... To them God has chosen to make known among the Gentiles the glorious riches of this mystery, which is Christ in you, the hope of glory. (Colossians 1:24-27)*

I don't need to whine about it, but I am, in my own real body, having an eternal life. Sometimes it hurts! I am not just in a "spiritual" place where everything is already happy and sanitized and free from the effects of sin. Just like Jesus became incarnate, a follower's flesh is Spirit-filled. Just like the Lord's love is bloody, so is ours. We have been sent into a dirty, daily, sweaty, struggle called life in Christ. It is my joy to bring the revelation of God into my every day life, which is not always happy or even pretty. My faith is not an abstract, "spiritual" concept, and my life is not an aspiration waiting to live up to its image. I'm not applied text or imagined perfection. I am a new self in Christ, living into myself in my own time and place, a self that is the restored image of God as seen in the face of Jesus.

That sounds pretty serious for as goofy as my friends and I can be. And there will be enough goofiness in this chapter to make sure you understand just how serious God needs to be to become one with us! For instance, He has to watch TV with us and listen to us argue whether Steve McQueen is important or not. Life in Christ is not just happening somewhere else we might get to someday, it is also happening in the cineplex and on the Schuylkill. And even though Jesus understands that his main allies are actually you and me, as weird as that might be, He's committed to that partnership. Jesus is not looking over our shoulders for someone he'd *really* like to meet. He wants to get with all of us. Matt Damon and Keanu Reeves can get mentioned in the same breath as Jesus, just like your name and mine. Jesus will be among all of us for the next few pages, and St. Patrick will bring him along with him at the end, too.

## The message has a body

If God had thought it best to merely send a text message announcing his ultimate step in the redemption of humankind, he could have sent it and signed it "JC." Or I suppose he could have sent some spam for those "with the programs to receive it" with a subject line like: *Visit Jesus at www.Jesus.com!* (BTW — as we speak, Jesus.com is a gay-inclusive church, Jesus.org is a site for Christian content, and Jesus.net is a business selling Christian goods. So I guess Jesus will have to get another domain name, unless www.suffering-servant.com is taken by the time he gets around to it).

Instead of texting or spamming, God came himself. This astounding act of humility and strategy is one of the great scandals of being a Christian in the 21st century. Madeline L'Engle writes of the incarnation we celebrate at Christmas time (if we remember to do that): *"This is the irrational season, when love blooms bright and wild, had Mary been filled with reason, there'd have been no room for the child."* A lot of people don't get the incarnation, even after they get the word explained to them. And a lot more don't want to.

But the message came in a body and it comes in my personal body, and it keeps coming in the body of Christ, the church. If we're evangelists, the incarnation is how we begin, just like God began in Jesus. If we followers have any sense of God's strategy, we are not walking arguments, as if only minds get saved. We reveal Jesus incarnationally, with a whole life that speaks and looks and feels like our Lord.

Here I go talking about "so many Christians" but *so many*

◄ A CIRCLE OF HOPE

Christians follow the "great commission" to make disciples out of all the people groups of the world (Matthew 28:16-20) and they do it as if all they have to do is get people to sit down for a class or a movie to "teach them everything I have commanded you." The Matthew 28 version might make that seem plausible, but there is more than one rendition of the great commission that defines our "family business." The one in John might be even clearer. It boils down the ongoing story of Jesus, the incarnation of God, into two sentences:

*"As the Father has sent me, I am sending you." And with that he breathed on them and said, "Receive the Holy Spirit." (John 20:21)*
Or it would be good to follow this pattern,

*When the time had fully come, God sent his Son, born of a woman, born under law, to redeem those under law, that we might receive the full rights of sons. Because you are sons, God sent the Spirit of his Son into our hearts, the Spirit who calls out, "Abba, Father." (Galatians 4:4-6)*

And this gives good direction, too:

*A new command I give you: Love one another. As I have loved you, so you must love one another. By this all men will know that you are my disciples, if you love one another. (John 13:34-35)*

The message needs to be revealed, and it is best revealed incarnationally. The character of what we continue to do with Jesus as part of his redemption project is all about animating breath, impregnating Spirit, demonstrable love.

Jesus is not revealed in a vacuum. He entered the world-as-it-was as a man, and he even more fully enters the world-as-it-is through the body of Christ, His church. The family business of God and his children is the restoration of creation's relationship with the Creator. It is a challenging business. It's not that people can't get the concept of Jesus in their head as much as they can't get the life of Jesus walking around in their life.

When we are giving people the good news of Jesus and inviting them into the body of Christ, some practices grow authentic Jesus-followers better than others. The most resilient, most representative

Christians are those who get baked in a Christian oven until they are done, or dipped in the solvent of the Spirit until their coating is gone, or bathed in the mineral springs of love until the hardness in their heart is loosened. When people join in our covenant, we give them a chance to tell us why they want to do it. Quite often we hear a story about being a part of the congregation long before they decided to be a Jesus-follower, much less an "out" member of the community!

The incarnation of Jesus in the world, the church, is elemental to His ongoing strategy for reformation:

*I have given them the glory that you gave me, that they may be one as we are one: I in them and you in me. May they be brought to complete unity to let the world know that you sent me and have loved them even as you have loved me."* (John 17:22-23)

Jesus knew that people need to rub up against glory to get some. They need to live in a body of people, experience a safe place of love, and acclimate to an environment charged with God's Spirit to be brought to glory. They need to sunbathe in forgiveness, soak in their rights as children, osmosize the sense of family that comes with being one with the Father. That's why the best teaching of all-Jesus-commands is incarnational — it comes in a body, it is organically grown in the soil of Spirit-seeded humanity, it is caught as much as taught as a result of living in the Christ-centered community. That's what we are trying to perfect....against all odds.

Strangely enough, the pop culture that's been forming for the last fifty years repeatedly demonstrates our yearning to get the Life in our lives. So don't be surprised at all the references to it as we check out seven challenges we feel as we try to reveal Jesus incarnationally. The world into which Jesus is coming is-as-it-is *now* — and it is a world of image, a world formed by advertising and propaganda, a world in which the democracy of thought is prized. The following thoughts on how the world is now won't even begin to answer the questions they raise about living with the Lord in such a world. But maybe we can get Jesus to shed some light on the challenges as we're talking. He's among us.

# 1. Overcoming Fake

Authentic children of God incarnate Jesus in their own bodies and in the bodies we call churches. This sets them apart and almost makes them illegal! The very idea that someone might be *more real* than someone else is pretty much considered immoral these days. As a result of this prevailing "morality," Christians sometimes feel guilty for thinking that having a life that reveals Jesus is important, since someone will undoubtedly label their attitude arrogant or even oppressive!

Americans have been taught for decades to make sure everyone is tolerated. *Will and Grace* (complete with their ironically religious names) was the TV primer on this for years. If you want to have a multicultural democracy, tolerance is a good thing. Christians have generally gone along with this so-called tolerance and made it a centerpiece of their morality, too. So what has happened is that inauthentic Christians are tolerated, too. If someone is wearing a Christian costume, and says they are they're Christian, then it must be received as true. Mormons work hard to get mainstreamed this way. All sorts of pastors don't believe Jesus rose from the dead, really — but don't question them! Christianity can all happen in someone's mind and what they do with their body doesn't make all that much difference.

In fairness, the Bible does say if a person says, "Jesus is Lord," it is an authenticating mark (1 Cor. 12:1-3). But we would be hard-pressed to find anyone who actually knew Jesus who thought being a follower of Jesus was just a matter of giving Him a shout out when you accepted your MTV Video Music Award for what amounts to shaking your moneymaker on screen in his name. A follower is a mind/soul/heart/body walking in the footsteps of the master. She does what the master is doing.

And what the master is doing is all about giving life to the next person He runs into. Life is not arising from molecular interaction, to be left undisturbed so it can develop, it is coming from the Giver of life. What is the Giver, incarnate in the world, doing all day? Jesus is wandering around meeting up with people, chatting, doing other people's jobs with them, making appointments to eat lunch with rich oppressors and have dinner with his opponents. He is who he is and he is open to give himself to the next person he meets.

An authentic church is like that, too: here for the next person to connect to God's Spirit incarnate in the world. An awful lot of churches aren't "here" at all; they live in a complex, a construct, or a concordance. A lot more are only here as long as they supply what the attendees expect is in it for them. So many people have run into these illegitimate babies that they are suspicious when they run into the real thing.

## 2. Being Important

God shows up in a body to redeem the world. God breathes new life like his into me and I am sent out to do my part in the project. The whole church, in its local renditions and its worldwide manifestation, is a big body of Christ — each part working as best it can to fill up what is left to complete in the family business. What an honor!

What a mess!

Why in the world does God want us so responsible for everything he is trying to accomplish? Like C. S. Lewis put it, it is a great "weight of glory." But we have been made that responsible.

I wish we thought of ourselves as that important. We are the amoeba of God! We are something like *The Blob* — possibly the best incarnation metaphor, ever. In my opinion, post-WW2 pop culture blossomed into *The Blob* in 1958, starring a young Steve McQueen (if you've never heard of him, at least you know I think he is famous). The poster for the sci-fi movie said, "Indescribable... indestructible... insatiable. The Blob!" The plot? An alien life-form lands in a small town. The teenagers who see it try to warn people, but no one listens to them (not to teenagers in the 50's, of course!). All the while The Blob is getting bigger, bloated on the blood of its victims. What I like about The Blob (rarely afforded protagonist status, mainly because it eats people), is that it knows who it is and does what a Blob should do. We could learn a lesson as the amoeba of God. The Blob has a purpose and relentlessly fulfills it. Like us, its nature is to incorporate humans. The Blob is too self-interested, of course, but it's just as messy as we are as it goes about its business (and there are a few other differences as well, but you get the idea).

People react to the church like people reacted to the Blob. It is indescribable, so I'll ignore it. It is indestructible, so I will rebel against it. It is insatiable so I will protect myself from being swallowed. Understandable. But the poor Blob! I mean, the poor Amoeba of God! It delivers God's truth, strength, and love. We don't want to let how messy it looks detract from its relevance!

## 3. Taking Time

Being incarnational by nature, is all about humans relating to humans — not just thought to thought or institution to adherent. Faith is personal — not just private, as many think. Following Jesus isn't about believing abstractions or not; faith has flesh and blood and lives in real time.

Such a human-to-human process of working with God in his redemption project is anything but instant. A person will not form a sustainable new life in the time it takes to walk down the aisle in response to a message or in the time the glow lasts after a podcast is over. As practitioners of this time-consuming means of redemption, we know our love to love, friend to friend commitment will take a long time to make the impact Jesus would like to make. It may never "happen" at all. But we are going to happen, nonetheless, because just like Jesus is who he is, so are we.

For instance, some people we have met are downright mentally ill. If you tell them something is black, they might tell you it is white because they really think it is. They are not being ornery. It just takes a while. It is said that one in four homeless mothers in Philadelphia have been sexually abused as a child in some way. Those dear people tend to mistrust. It will take a while. About 7% of the population are alcoholics, and twice as many have been raised by one, a figure said to be higher among people with certain ancestries common to Philly. They are often filled with shame and act in secret. It takes time.

Being a safe place with a mission requires an appreciation of the commitment it takes to embrace people like a body and hold on. It takes having discernment about when to let go or cast out and when to receive back. Better work is done by patient erosion than some kind of upheaval. You've got to really be someone and really be there. Without a warm body with them, sin-addicted people revert to the habits of their hearts and minds that kept them "safe" before they had a shot at knowing God face to face.

## 4. Staying Available

While we are sampling hall-of-fame pop culture, let's remember Mr. Whipple. Actor Dick Wilson made 504 commercials, a whole career, from 1964 to the early 90's, as Mr. Whipple. In 1978 he was the best known American after Richard Nixon and Billy Graham. He was the voice of propriety, telling us, "Please don't squeeze the Charmin," that sensuous TP (which he found irresistible himself). The culture is longing for squeezable and the advertisers know it.

The church has not known this as well as the ad men. While Whipple sold TP, the church could be advertised as anything but squeezable. It still has statues of Mary, an intricate approach to Bible study, and a stringent morality that has everyone squeezing around in secret and feeling guilty about needing to be squeezed at all! The Christian songs are squishier these days, that's true, but the singers can still be pretty self-conscious, veering from virginal to Madonna and being criticized for either. And what could be more remote and less Jesus-like than a giant, jumbotron picture of your pastor *acting* squeezable in front of 10,000 people? What could be less like a follower of Jesus than finding your identity as an avatar on-line looking for a Christian date?

Jesus is best revealed when he is squeezable. That's why Circle of Hope keeps the congregations to 200 and pushes everyone into a cell. Christianity is face to face, person to person. I think people *should* be skeptical if our message does not originate from a community that demonstrates the love of Christ — and people *are* skeptical. They don't need a Christianized version of enlightenment materialism and technological domination; they've got great TP. They need to meet God.

## 5. Making Connections

What is on screen these days is about the only culture we all share. Sometimes, surprisingly, it erupts with the longings that Jesus would like to soothe. Our culture is crying out for Jesus to be revealed incarnationally: breathing, present, approachable, loving, demonstrable. The younger people are, the more bereft of connectedness they seem to be, since they've been stuck alone in front of a monitor, locked away by terrified parents who are at work, deprived of the joy of building or planting or even playing in an unstructured way. The media often channels these unrealized desires and plays them back like a soothing itch cream that doesn't really cure the rash.

*Stuck on You*, the Farrelly Brothers comedy, is a charming way of approaching the itch to be connected — the movie is something of an incarnation message without Jesus. Conjoined twins, Matt Damon and Greg Kinnear, go to LA to advance Greg's film career, meet Cher and other girls, and decide to get a surgeon to separate them. But once apart, they find out that being together is who they are meant to be. It is such a countercultural statement! Most psychologists, even, only have "Get used to being alone" as the antidote to the depressing loneliness so many of us feel. But here the Farrelly brothers are celebrating mutuality.

In such an individualistic age, just being together (what's more being the church) is a countercultural statement. From the outside, people wonder if a community is a cult, if sharing is codependence, if morality is oppression, if accountability is even legal! Being real, being in love with more than your sexual partner, staying, having an open-ended commitment is going to keep seeming weird, but attractive.

## 6. Being Planted

I think the most striking scene in *The Matrix* is not one of the fight scenes (even the one with the slow-mo bullets!), it is the one in which Keanu/Neo is rescued from the pod where he has been functioning as a battery for the matrix. His tubes blast off his back, he is flushed down his "birth canal," picked up by the rebels and Morpheus says, *"Welcome to the real world."*

Neo asks, *"Am I dead?"*

That sounds like becoming a Christian, too. More and more people have a legitimate fear that we are all becoming slaves to the huge systems that keep spooning out bits of sustenance if we keep typing things into the massive data base that empowers them and defines us. Escaping it feels like dying to a former self.

The incarnation of Jesus in the world is the opposite of being incorporated into a machine. He is an actual, living being fed from the Spirit of God and in touch with the joys built into creation. He is not an alien factory that needs more human effort and energy to produce illusions. Jesus in His body *is*. That body grows like a plant in the field, not like a conglomerate in what we call "the corporate world."

Being an organism requires a shift from the perverse paradigm that dominates us. We know organization, but we've lost organism. Dominated by the machine one can be under the illusion that she makes all the choices — you take the job or quit it, you buy the product or not. In the organism, one is part of what is growing and God is supplying the growth — he moves with how the Spirit is moving like an aspen in the wind. When Jesus was telling his followers to consider what being a lily is like (Matthew 6), I don't think he was just being colorful or impractical. I think he wanted to save our lives.

## 7. Revealing Jesus

Jesus is best revealed incarnationally because it is hard to see something that is not a body. Sigmund Freud and his gang of secularizers tried to make sure we all thought that the *real* world was material, that the *illusory* world was "spiritual" and that the twain did not meet. Many followers have been driven to have a "private" faith, since they fearfully, but stubbornly, hold on to something the "experts" say is no more than a "superstition," or cling to something the anthropology prof teaches is no more than one's personal version of ancestor worship.

When the second President Bush was asked, during a presidential debate, how his faith would affect his policymaking, he first assured everyone that his faith is "very private." I'm not sure that private faith is Christian at all. It is more like having an ice cream preference. Being incarnational makes faith in Jesus naked and unashamed. Faith is right out there in our lives, in our bodies, in our Body, and in whatever debate we get into.

We don't have sacred and secular, private and public, personal and abstract "lives." We have one life that has been given to us by God in the work of Jesus. Everywhere we go, Jesus goes with us. Everyone we meet meets Jesus in us. It is the same mentality the Celtic-based church understood so well and taught, up until the Rome-based authorities took over. The famous prayer attributed to St. Patrick (the "breastplate" prayer, it is called) speaks so well of having one life — and of Jesus making and directing it. Here's part of it:

*For my shield this day*
*A mighty power:*
*The Holy Trinity!*
*Affirming threeness,*
*Confessing oneness,*
*In the making of all*
*Through love….*

# REVEALING JESUS INCARNATIONALLY

*Christ beside, Christ before me;*
*Christ behind me, Christ within me;…*
*Christ in my lying, my sitting, my rising;*
*Christ in the heart of all who know me,*
*Christ on the tongue of all who meet me,*
*Christ in the eye of all who see me,*
*Christ in the ear of all who hear me.*

Saying that prayer again and sensing the power of God with me, feeling confident that I can represent Jesus, that I can actually live in Christ, makes me remember those critical young women again having an awkward, anguished conversation about worship. Perhaps they just did not sense that reality of God's presence behind all that whining!! Or maybe they did sense it and just didn't want to go the way of incarnation — which definitely *isn't* tidy and *isn't* always happy. It is like God in me and me in God

It is scandalous, isn't it? We might perversely prefer a religion that is a work of art, not an ongoing revelation. But God's deepest work of art is not a beautiful baby perfectly captured on canvas, it is the beautiful baby in the manger. We're vulnerable like that baby — accessible, hurtable, soiled. We might passionately prefer an experience that gives us a permanent feeling of triumph. But God's deepest work of power was not a shock and awe treatment like the world respects, it was Jesus emptying himself and being sent as a servant, one with others, connected, empathetic, compelled by love, suffering. We're trying to be like that, too, alive with the Spirit breathed into our Body, being a kingdom that is organic and grows like the creation — killable and resurrectable.

CHAPTER 4

# Moving with What the Spirit is Doing Next
*The Story: Jesus and Philip the pioneers, Acts 8*

Imposed hardship can be a quick teacher! So I learned some good lessons about following Jesus by leading high-schoolers through the wilderness of the High Sierras on backpacking trips. The most instructive part of our treks usually came on the very first day, when the packs were heaviest and the feet were softest. We hiked from the desert side of the mountains where the trailheads are at lower elevations and the first decent campsites are about eight miles straight up. For beginners and the out-of-shape, the first hard day on the trail meant blisters and exhaustion, to go along with the sunburn and flies. Mucho complaining, and worse, ensued.

Keeping the group together and moving along was a challenge! There was always a jackrabbit 16-year-old guy in the lead proving his manhood, and there was always a 32-year-old woman leader (who just *had* to come) sitting on a rock at the back saying, *"Oh, just leave me.(pant, pant)... I'll catch up with you (wheeze)"*

There are always the pioneers and there are always the settlers.

Usually, once we got to the first stop on a trip, the discovery of who were pioneers and who were settlers became even more evident. Inevitably, we would get to a great campsite and a whole bunch would want to settle there for the whole week! It didn't matter that our final destination was the most beautiful lake ever; it didn't even matter that we would never get back to our car in time to go home if we didn't keep moving! They just wanted to stay, rest, and get comfortable. There was usually a smaller bunch who wanted to put their blisters back in their boots and trek on toward our goal. Thank God there are always a few!

## On the Road, Like Phillip

Those backpacking experiences helped me learn how to try to lead Circle of Hope. Our church is a pioneer church in a world of settlers. We know that some of us, compared to others, seem like we are sitting at the back of the pack. But as a whole, we are people called out to go on the journey with Jesus and we have responded. We have launched out into eternal life, believing that "over the rise" there is a better way, maybe the most authentic way, certainly the next way to live. We have a destination, and if it is hard to get there, then it is hard — but we need to get there. We are moving with what the Spirit is doing next. We are trying to keep up with Jesus as He leads us.

Some, of course, think of us as a jack-rabbit, young church that will be sitting on a rock once everyone grows up. We'll see. What I hope is that we are among those few pioneers God keeps finding to go with the latest way he wants to express himself in the latest culture that has arisen. No matter what *is*, there is always what's *next*. We may be trying to relate to what's about to become normal, but we are reacting from the most ancient of impulses.

Moving with the Spirit is hardly a new idea. In every era, God has to find people to travel with him as he is moving through time with us and leading people into eternity. One of my favorite examples of this Spirit-inspired impulse is Phillip, whose exploits are recorded in the New Testament book of Acts. His responsiveness has made Philip an example for us for 2000 years. As a church, we are called out to be like him and like the people who have been like him ever since.

## MOVING WITH WHAT THE SPIRIT IS DOING NEXT

For Philip, what's next began after one of the leaders of the first church made a very aggressive speech before the Jewish leadership council. A general outbreak of persecution erupted in Jerusalem. People fled for their lives. As a result, believers spread all over the country. Just as you'd expect, wherever the believers landed, new people heard the story of Jesus and new congregations began to spring up.

If you throw a follower of Jesus (a person filled with the Spirit of God) into a reasonably fertile spiritual field (some place God has been plowing) they will reproduce themselves and produce another rendition of the church. They are the presence of the future. Wherever Philip and the rest of the first church ended up, God made himself known through them and something new happened with new people. We say that the church exists for those yet to join. So when the first church in Jerusalem got scattered, the church did just what you'd expect. You have to wonder if God was involved, helping to push the situation in Jerusalem to its breaking point, so that people *had* to get out of their exciting, getting-comfy, new church and go meet the next people. Regardless, Philip finds himself sown like a seed into the surprisingly fertile territory of Samaria. It says:

*Those who had been scattered preached the word wherever they went. Philip went down to a city in Samaria and proclaimed the Christ there. When the crowds heard Philip and saw the miraculous signs he did, they all paid close attention to what he said. With shrieks, unclean spirits came out of many, and many paralytics and cripples were healed. So there was great joy in that city…(Acts 8:4- 8)*

Philip had little choice about doing something new, since persecution drove him out of Jerusalem. But once he got to unexplored territory, he still had some choices o make about whether he would go with what God wanted to do through him now. You might relate to how challenged he was.

- Chances are, he already liked what he had going in Jerusalem and here he was in a new place doing something new and uncalled for. He had an *emotional* challenge. I might have felt like I got a raw deal, at least felt a little afraid, most likely felt

sulky — not totally enthused about demonstrating the Spirit of Jesus.
- He was in Samaria where Jerusalemites didn't go. There was an ethnic prejudice thing going on. He had a *social* challenge. Philip could have shut down, put his blinders on, felt distant or disgusted and trudged right through Samaria without touching a soul — going with the way things are, not with what is next.
- What's more, the people in Samaria didn't know what it was like to have the Holy Spirit incarnate and exercising power. They had a religion they thought was OK. Philip had a *religious* challenge. He had to go against their sense of what is to introduce what is next. He could have not said a thing and just moved into their sense of what is normal and settled down in Sychar — free from being pushed into further risks by faith in Jesus.

There were a lot of reasons not to go where Jesus leads, not to do what Jesus does, not to go further when Jesus calls. But Philip was a pioneer. He had a sense of how the world works that was different from the people he was meeting and soon the people he met also had a new way of seeing things. They met Jesus and saw a whole new future to live into. It says they received the evidence of the new life he brought with great joy.

## Flexible Hearts

That's the way it worked that time. But what's next is not always received with great joy. For instance, I often talk to people from religious backgrounds that have a glorious history, and they often think of "next" as bad. They don't think what they have is broken and they are sure that if you go back to what was, whatever problem you have will be fixed. Catholics go back to the 500's. Anabaptists go back to the 1500's. Methodists go back to the 1700's. Assemblies of God go back to 1910 or so, Circle of Hope goes back to 1996. People love their style and they get settled in it. I was a history major in college and I developed a deep appreciation for the Jesus-followers of the past who lived brilliant applications of life in Christ in their eras. I think we'd be fools not to take what is good from our ancestors in Christ and hold on to it. We are a transhistorical body, after all. But rather than refining what others invented, it is more important to trust God's presence and move with what the Spirit is doing next. That's exactly what all the pioneers who started the movements that people love did to start the movements!

Pioneers of the past all caused similar problems for the settlers they disrupted. We cause problems, too. Here is a small example from the history of Circle of Hope. We've often had some awkward dialogue with people from the "evangelical" tradition who think we aren't teaching the Bible. It is not so much that we are not Bible people, but we don't often teach in a format that some people like — they don't think we are doing it unless we do it the way they were told is orthodox. In the past 50 years, especially, many pastors conformed how they teach the Bible to how people teach other subjects and called it orthodox. They began to extract "principles" from the "source material." They dissected the raw material of the Bible into components and reassembled them according to a unifying theme. Since many people think that way, it is no big surprise that many Christians like their Bible served up in a modern bowl. They want me and others to talk about the Bible according to the post-enlightenment paradigm they were taught in the churches they used to know and according to the pattern they experience in a lot of other institutions like schools and laboratories.

But I want to be like Philip, show up in Samaria, and help create a whole new church with a whole next story. I'd like the story to be based on the presence of Jesus with us and not just on a sampling of the thinking of other people or on the principles of a successful franchise from the past. Here's how it happened:

*An angel of the Lord said to Philip, "Go south to the road—the desert road—that goes down from Jerusalem to Gaza." So he started out, and on his way he met an Ethiopian eunuch, an important official in charge of all the treasury of Candace, queen of the Ethiopians. This man had gone to Jerusalem to worship, and on his way home was sitting in his chariot reading the book of Isaiah the prophet. The*

Spirit told Philip, "Go to that chariot and stay near it."

Then Philip ran up to the chariot and heard the man reading Isaiah the prophet. "Do you understand what you are reading?" Philip asked.

"How can I," he said, "unless someone explains it to me?" So he invited Philip to come up and sit with him.

The eunuch was reading this passage of Scripture: "He was led like a sheep to the slaughter, and as a lamb before the shearer is silent, so he did not open his mouth. In his humiliation he was deprived of justice. Who can speak of his descendants? For his life was taken from the earth." (Isaiah 53:7, 8)

The eunuch asked Philip, "Tell me, please, who is the prophet talking about, himself or someone else?" Then Philip began with that very passage of Scripture and told him the good news about Jesus. (Acts 8:26-35)

Before long the official wants to be baptized. He probably took the message of Jesus back to Ethiopia and sowed the seeds that grew up into one of the first Christian nations.

I would like to have a story like that told about me, or about any of us. Philip is so available to the Spirit! An angel can speak to him! He will move according to what the angel says. He will run up to the chariot of an official. You have to have a flexible heart to do that.

## The Invasion of Change Opportunities

A flexible heart is often hard-won, as in the case of Philip, I think. Pioneers don't always choose to be one — and when they do choose, they don't know what they are getting into. The situation requires adaptation. The presence of Jesus will most likely be doing some recreating. Pioneering is not predictable. One of my ancestors came from the slums of Liverpool in the 1840s to join the Latter-Day Saints in the promised land of Utah. But once he got to Iowa and realized that Brigham Young had solidified the doctrine of polygamy, he said, "No way!" So he ended up farming near Council Bluffs, where my mother was eventually born. He caught a vision (however loony it might have been) in England, but the reality ended up a lot different in Iowa. Pioneering can be like that.

When we got started in Philadelphia, we decided we would rely on Jesus to make it happen. We had some nice plans, of course. But they included "praying up" what we needed to survive. So, for instance, one of our first lofty goals was to meet a sympathetic realtor! I was calling about office possibilities and ended up in an apartment over Eddie's Tattoos. But another realtor I had contacted remembered my story and called me back with a possibility for a meeting space. This nice, Jewish man became a good friend who constructed a lease deal that was so cheap it was a marvel! How God gets things done is usually surprising. I often wonder how he stays in business.

Philip was probably surprised at how his life turned out, too. He probably thought becoming a Christian and being part of the radical Jerusalem church was wild enough. But his life continued to be invaded by opportunities to move with the Spirit. Philip might have been from the slums of Jerusalem, as many of the first believers were. He had probably already become an outcast from his family when he gave his loyalty to Jesus. He'd already experienced a lot of change. But then the church was persecuted by the authorities and their mobs and he ended up homeless. He was run out of town, and became a fugitive. Then an angel tells him (an unlikely occurrence, to say the least) to go up to a chariot (a dangerous war machine), driven by a high-ranking official (total class problems, plus the official is black — possible race issues). And he does it. That's moving with what the Spirit is doing next!

That should be typical of Christians. If the revelation of God invades our consciousness in Jesus Christ and we grasp the opportunity to follow him in his death, resurrection and life, and therefore enjoy a renewed relationship with God, Spirit to spirit — what else would we do but live with some kind of confident abandon? For Jesus-followers it is perfectly natural to invade the world with opportunity just like we were invaded! What we do may not be so extraordinary that Luke wants to write it down in the book of Acts.

## A CIRCLE OF HOPE

But there would be a story about *something* to tell.

A person with a flexible heart may be called to do things that seem somewhat impulsive — like going where God wants you to go, ending up in Samaria and then down on the road to Egypt. People all over the world are doing just that, and the pioneers are among us, too — God always finds someone! For instance, Circle of Hope's wandering mission team, called the Psalters, spent a lot of time on the road in the past few years looking for opportunities to invade settlements with the opportunity they bring to move with the Spirit in worship. They try to be respectfully disruptive. But the call is clear in their songs:

*Revolution, come free us,*
*Holy brother us. Desert wanderers*
*Have no place to call home.*

*Physician, come heal us,*
*Holy mender us. Blind old lepers*
*Cannot find our way home.*

*Compassion, come save us,*
*Holy lover us. Warmongers*
*Ruined this place we call home.*

*Refugee, just like me,*
*Please don't leave.*
*You're our only… home*

The opportunity for change is not just about creating something new. New is not necessarily better, although I usually like the newest variations on Pepsi or Reese's Peanut Butter cups — and I really liked how they put chocolate on a Payday recently. People (like me) can like new for the sake of newness. But the pioneers we admire are doing next, not new. Life in Christ may seem new in territory where it has not been fully known, but it is older than all the stories.

We're carrying it into the future, not inventing something. It is like new, but its home is in eternity.

## A Pioneer Church in a World of Settlers

It is always a settler vs. a pioneer mentality. They definitely compete. The mentalities get mad at each other — Aunt Eller needs to sing "the farmer and the cowman should be friends" about every other day. The farmer is always fencing in the cowman, so everyone in *Oklahoma* is on edge. Having said that, let me admit, at this juncture, that we know this extended metaphor we are working on, breaks down if you look at it too closely. There are farmer pioneers and cowman settlers, in the Spirit. We're using the metaphor to see if we can maintain a feeling for moving on and not settling in inappropriately. We're settled in eternity, which means we are moving on through this era. We were settled in self-destruction and we are on our way into our fullness, so we need to resist the temptation to stay put.

The need to keep developing into what is next is why I was glad when what is now the "Broad and Washington" congregation got disrupted in 2005. Right after we sent off a new congregation, we lost our fabulous lease and *had* to move with what the Spirit is doing next. So often we have to *choose* to move. But this time, like Philip, we ended up dislocated. As tiresome as it was — inconvenient, anxiety-ridden and expensive, too, I think it might have been our best shot at getting refined enough to stay on the road for another decade.

We were settling into a pleasant Circle of Hopeness, full of hard-won and now long—held friendships, familiar patterns, secure tracks of avoidance. It is hard not to think that God had a hand in depriving us of our place. People like to settle; Circle of Hope likes to settle. People like to sit down on the trail because they have gone far enough. I often think that is how Nebraska got settled at all, because Oregon was just too far! The kids said, "Build me a sod house, Dad," so he did.

The tendency to settle is one good reason to have all the trail boss-cell leaders we have who are determined multiply another cell before too long — otherwise we'd all be tempted to settle in and stop being pioneers. We'd get a couple of friends and start fearing the loss of them because we were going to be making some more friends! Jesus would be riding off into the dawn without us, while we were looking into the sunset, all comfy on the front porch of our settledness.

## The Pioneer Church in a Nutshell

At times we have been accused of beating the pioneers vs. settlers metaphor to death. That might be true. We could have used *catacomb vs. basilica* Christians (cue up the Gladiator soundtrack). We could have used *tabernacle vs. temple* Christians (great pictures from the Sinai). We could have used *guerilla vs. empire* churches (a little Latin American motif). We could have used *pilgrim vs. cathedral* faith (that might have a nice Celtic ring). One picture can speak a thousand words, which has to be why Jesus painted so many.

Maybe we'll get to all those pictures. I always go back to Brennan Manning's very American analogy when I am thinking about who we are (Lion and Lamb or Wes Seeliger's Frontier Theology). We are pioneers, not settlers — or we aren't like Philip, and not much like Jesus, who Hebrews says is the "pioneer and perfecter of our faith" (12:1, TNIV). Unless we bear the pain of moving into new territory until we reach the final frontier, we're not much like Jesus who has gone through death to life and is continuing with us as we get to the end of the trail ourselves, and into our eternal what's next.

I don't leave you with this analogy so you can merely compare yourself to the ideal Christian and prove yourself wanting — *"On a scale of one to ten, am I a 5 or an 8 pioneer?"* I leave it so we can meditate on the picture and install an image of who Jesus is calling us to be. We were settled in this world and now we are called into eternity. We get settled in our habits and Jesus keeps calling us to grow into what is next. We are each on our own journey and as a people we are on a journey together. We are pioneering this time and going with what he is doing now. As a result we are bringing the

## MOVING WITH WHAT THE SPIRIT IS DOING NEXT

presence of the future with us wherever we end up.

We can be *settlers or pioneers*.

If we are *settlers* we'll tend to see life as a possession to be carefully tended and guarded.

If we are *pioneers* we will be more likely to see life as something wild, a gift we are given, an opportunity to travel with Jesus, to grow, and to serve the need of the moment.

*Settler stories* gravitate toward trying to answer all the questions, define and housebreak some sort of Supreme Being, and establish the status quo as something that will be good forever.

*Pioneer stories* talk about what it means to receive the strange gift of life and live it. They are about looking for maps through new territory.

If you imagine old sets built for Wild West movies on Hollywood back lots, it might help you to keep going with this picture…

The *settler's idea of the church*, is the territory courthouse. It is the center of town life. The old stone structure dominates the town square. Its windows are small and this makes things dark inside. Within the courthouse walls, records are kept, taxes collected, trials held for bad guys. The courthouse is the settler's symbol of law, order, stability, and—most important—security. Jesus is like the mayor with an office on the top floor. His eagle eye ferrets out the smallest details of town life.

The *pioneer's idea of the church*, is the covered wagon. It's a house on wheels, always on the move. The covered wagon is where the pioneers eat, sleep, fight, love, and die. It bears the marks of life and movement—it creaks, it is scarred with arrows, it is bandaged with bailing wire. The covered wagon is always where the action is. It moves toward the future and doesn't bother to glorify its own ruts. The old wagon isn't comfortable, but the pioneers don't mind. They are more into adventure than comfort. Besides, Jesus is the trail boss, and he keeps things going, even as he helps with the problems of moving though uncharted territory.

When the *settler looks at a Christian* she sees a settler. She fears the open, unknown frontier. Her concern is to stay on good terms with the mayor and keep the law so she doesn't get into trouble and get thrown out of town. "Safety first" is her motto. To her the courthouse is a symbol of security, peace, order, and happiness.

When the *pioneer looks at a Christian* she sees a pioneer. She is a person of daring, hungry for new life. She rides hard and knows how to use a gun when necessary. The pioneer feels sorry for the settlers and tries to tell them of the joy and fulfillment of life on the trail. She dies with her boots on.

For a *settler, to have faith* means trusting in the safety of the town: obeying the laws, keeping your nose clean, believing the mayor is in the courthouse.

For a *pioneer, to have faith* means living with a spirit of adventure: being ready to move out, risking everything on the trail, obeying the restless voice of the trail boss.

One twenty-four year old shared some reactions to this online: "All my life, all I've done is try and simplify my life and settle, which in effect has really led me to isolation and depression. To be clear, simplicity is good. But simplicity for a settler really means less of everything, including authentic relationships and love. For a pioneer, however, simplicity means focus, determination, patience, and obedience. That's what I long for. Waking up with a purpose, rather than waking up with an empty schedule and calling that simplicity!"

In *settler theology*, sin is breaking one of the town's ordinances. Salvation is living close to home and hanging around the courthouse.

In *pioneer theology*, sin is wanting to turn back. Salvation is being more afraid of sterile town life than of death on the trail.

Jesus is a *pioneer*. He's not just moving for the sake of moving. He stayed until his mission called him to go. But there is no doubt that destiny is pulling on him. He was a rock that was happening. Likewise we are living stones.

Philip was his *pioneer* follower. He wasn't just trying something new. He was not just into extreme experiences trying to find something to feel. He chose to go with Jesus and Jesus chose to lead him into

## MOVING WITH WHAT THE SPIRIT IS DOING NEXT

some world-changing opportunities.

Circle of Hope is a *pioneer* church. It is not that we collected all the bungee-jumping types and made a church out of them. It is not that we can't stand the present or the past and prefer our own control on the future. We're all prone to settle like everyone else, and if we resist the impulse ourselves, all the children we are birthing will soon give us more motivation to build a fence around our world. But we decided to follow Jesus — that means personally, like Jesus is the living Lord whose Spirit continues to lead us.

Settlers don't always understand or appreciate our convictions. But our convictions give people a chance to experience true joy when they get a straight look at the Spirit at work in a people. We're not only surviving on this hostile frontier, we're invading it with the peace of Christ and leading many through it.

CHAPTER 5

# Going Deep with God
*The Story: Jesus walks on water, Matthew 13 and 14*

I have had a number of friends who are bi-polar in one way or another, meaning their brain chemistry disconnects them from "normal" feelings and behavior. All of these friends have also self-medicated in one way or another — alcohol being their anesthesia of choice. They found it difficult to cope with their highs and lows. They couldn't sacrifice the ecstasy and take their meds when they were manic, and they couldn't find the energy to take their meds when they were depressed. Zima took one of these friends off a mountain road and left him wedged, upside-down in the driver's seat, barely alive.

I sometimes wonder if the epidemic of drunkenness on college campuses is fueled by the sense of disconnection more and more people seem to feel. We're always trying to "get it together," but we're failing. A lot of people are trying to get drunk enough to get it together with someone *else*, and that doesn't relieve the feeling of disconnection for very long, either.

We can't connect in so many ways! But we want to. We can't get it together within ourselves or with others, much less with God. So we self-medicate. As a result, The U.S. is an addicted society, soaking up all the opiates Afghan warlords can export, foiling the "war on drugs" in Colombia and Peru and giving the North Koreans a constant client for black market marijuana. But does anyone really think any of the treatments are working?

So many people we meet in the Sunday meetings are empty, separated, lonely, shamed. They have often already dragged their burdens through other religious experiences and nothing has changed. The Church has not been a better solution than anything else. So often the best the Church can do is tell people to, "Look on the bright side," or, "Claim your prosperity." The Church even mimics the self-help gurus with, "Be self-reliant," or, "Follow these five steps to victorious living." A lot of Christians have perfected a behavior called "spiritual bypass" in which they use their spiritual principals as a mind/feeling-numbing way around what is *really* happening to them. They cruise by reality in a cloud of platitudes and rote praises. Sometimes "going to church" is a lot like getting a fix. The church can be just another pusher or a great enabler for another anesthesia of choice.

No church-person is trying to do anyone, harm, in general, but a lot of the Church's cures have been as bad as the dis-ease, or just another package for it. God has used a lot of very bad ways to draw us near, but I think he wishes he didn't have to start in negative territory when trying to establish a positive relationship with needy people. Faithful Christians have been born while watching a Christian infomercial! — but it is not likely that they stayed faithful by zoning out on further infomercials. So we try to discover better ways to teach each other.

The infomercial approach will tell people things like, "God will make a relationship with you that is very similar to your addictive relationship with Macy's" so you'll buy God. It might tell people that, "Whatever urge you have is what God wants to fulfill," so you'll get what you came looking for and tune in again (and send a check!). That has made a lot of people's situation even worse. So we have been trying to come up with ways to tell people the real truth that Jesus demonstrates.

Lots of people claim they have the "real truth" so you'll have to sort out whether what is coming next is good with God. But it seems pretty common-sensical. Merely alleviating someone's anxiety or medicating their disconnection rarely helps them along the way to God. We need to learn to suffer and we need to learn to suffer through. We need to go deep with God. Circle of Hope is here for that.

## Suffering through

So many of us are feeling a ton of anxiety right now! As I am writing, the country is reeling from the news that there was a conspiracy to blow up jets taking off from Heathrow bound for the U.S. Israel and Hezbollah are fighting. Iraq is splintering. Afghanistan is fraying. The U.S. consensus on our wars is disintegrating. The *whole world* is scary on top of what usually makes us unsure. Many people find themselves longing to connect. We feel a call from God and wonder how to answer:

*Why are you downcast, O my soul?*
*Why so disturbed within me?*
*Put your hope in God, for I will yet praise him,*
*my Savior and my God.*
*My soul is downcast within me;*
*therefore I will remember you…*
*Deep calls to deep in the roar of your waterfalls;*
*all your waves and breakers have swept over me.*
*(Psalm 42:5-7)*

When trouble comes we often realize that we don't have the resources with which to respond. Sometimes we see how our reactions keep us shallow and out of touch. We are depressingly disconnected when we desperately need to be in touch with God. When we wake up with anxiety in the dark, we want to confidently reach out our hands and be saved.

If these thoughts coming from the above psalm were slogans: "Go deep with God" or "Learn how to suffer through," they would be such a bad way to advertise God to disconnected Americans! Sometimes I wish we could boil things down into catchy phrases or a little booklet (*Depth for Dummies*) that would make everything seem easier. I have a couple of friends right now who are into Alcoholics Anonymous and have a slogan a minute — all basically sound. But Jesus needs to be behind Steps 1-2-3 or no one gets saved enough. Jesus drags us deeper than a pithy saying, and as a result, draws us through our own harrowing escape from slavery.

Three people in my cell recently quit their jobs to go deeper with God. It was an epidemic of conviction! It all got started when one quit because getting paid for delivering phone sex is just plain wrong. Another quit because making sure abusive parents can't harm their children is only good if you have a way for abusive parents to grow, and the government only punishes. One quit because music is who he is, even though entrepreneurship makes a lot of money. Suddenly, they all had no money. The suffering was disturbing. These days, new depth is being required of them. They are tempted to go back on "off" and do what it takes to get the money and alleviate their anxiety. We'll see where they put their hope.

## Jesus calling deep to deep

Jesus was tempted to disconnect, too. His story gives us more insight about what keeps us from going deep with God.

In Matthew 13 and 14 there is an account of a period in the life of Jesus in which God is having a difficult time. Being fully human, Jesus is developing in his understanding of who he is and what it is going to take to complete his mission and be fully himself. Like the rest of us, confusing forces are trying to get in his way.

The account starts with John the Baptist's death. King Herod, the ruler of Jesus' home territory of Galilee, imprisoned John for confronting him about his illegal marriage to Herodias, who was not only his brother's ex-wife, but also the daughter of his half-brother. Herodias's daughter was the famous Salome who asked for the head of John the Baptist on a platter and got it.

When Jesus heard the news that John had received the most recent version of capital punishment, it says he, *"withdrew by boat privately to a solitary place."* Jesus needed to be alone with God to consider what was happening. He needed to sort out his emotion, to listen, to decide. This was one of the worst things that ever happened to Jesus — John was dead: his cousin, his baptizer, the prophet, his forerunner. He must have felt very alone. I think he realized His time had come. He was now the one on whom everything depended.

*But* crowds of people followed him to the solitary place he sought. So he didn't get to be alone for long. He saw all the people and felt compassion for them. He loved them. He began to heal them. This is so like God, who could have stayed alone in the universe, but created people with whom to share love. God could have left us alone in our self-destruction, but he came in Jesus to lift us out. Even though Jesus needed to be alone with God, he served these people for hours. He was at it so long that it came time for the evening meal and everyone was still out in the boondocks. That was when the Lord fed 5000 with a few loaves and fish.

A very good thing followed a very bad thing. Within just a few hours, Jesus experienced the despair of losing John and the exhilaration of revealing God's love and power in a way he had never done before. A season ended and a new season began. He endured loss and gained a deeper sense of himself. Solitude happened in the middle. There is a lot to make of how Jesus suffered through.

## Getting in deep with Jesus getting in deep with us

Jesus needed to be alone with God. People often wonder, metaphysically, "If Jesus is God as a human — how can God need to get alone with God?" I'm not too metaphysical, meaning I may not be cut out for highly rational thinking and abstract philosophy, but let me try something. One way to understand how Jesus (God) can be talking to God, is to look at myself keeping track of my true self. There is a lot of inner dialogue going on in me. Entire parts of my person seem to be lost to me, at times. When I am silent and reflect, I often get reconnected. God is not the same as me, but I think there is some similarity when you see Jesus communing with God. He's a person keeping in connection within himself. We say we get "torn apart," or feel "disjointed." God got himself into situations that were difficult, too.

Whenever we go out the door in Philly, we need to do something to stay connected, to keep it real, to be centered. There are a lot of things that might tear us apart. Bullets fly and disturb the peace. People move in from all over the world and disrupt normality. Giant corporations build high rises next door and plow up neighborhoods. Nobody stops for a red light! — the whole enterprise just keeps moving. If Jesus had a hard time getting away so deep could connect to deep, we might have an even harder time! We need a lot of mentoring in the art of connecting with God. So it is great to see God-in-a-body doing what a body needs to do to connect when times are hard or confusing or challenging.

The account says that after the scraps from the miraculous meal were gathered up and the people were headed home, Jesus sent the disciples on a boat to the other side of the lake. *"After he had dismissed them, he went up on a mountainside by himself to pray."* (Matt 14:23, NIV)

He got into a solitary place again. He maintained the depth. In the middle of loss, and learning, and maybe even doubt, Jesus recovered the depth. After being invaded by thousands of people and loving his heart out doing powerful things to reveal God, he went deep. What happened next is so powerful, and is such a fundamental picture of our spiritual process, it bears another meditative reading:

*When evening came, he was there alone, but the boat was already a considerable distance from land, buffeted by the waves because the wind was against it. During the fourth watch of the night Jesus went out to them, walking on the lake. When the disciples saw him walking on the lake, they were terrified. "It's a ghost," they said, and cried out in fear.*

*But Jesus immediately said to them: "Take courage! It is I. Don't be afraid."*

*"Lord, if it's you," Peter replied, "tell me to come to you on the water."*

*"Come," he said.*

*Then Peter got down out of the boat, walked on the water and came toward Jesus. But when he saw the wind, he was afraid and, beginning to sink, cried out, "Lord, save me!"*

*Immediately Jesus reached out his hand and caught him. "You of little faith," he said, "why did you doubt?" And when they climbed into the boat, the wind died down.*

*Then those who were in the boat worshiped him, saying, "Truly you are the Son of God." (Matthew 14:23-33)*

"Why did you doubt, Peter?" Could it be that Jesus questioned Peter because he had just solidified his own triumph over doubt during his solitude? The death of his cousin, the new weight of responsibility, maybe even the temptation to fear his own death, might have made Jesus doubt. But instead of sinking with it, he rose to compassion and love and, out of the depths of God, fed 5000. Then he walked on water and called his friends to join him!

From this great piece of history, I think we should latch on to three things Peter and the gang learned from Jesus about going deep with God that day. There are ways to prevent sinking, ways to stay connected. It would be tempting to fixate on all the ways the disciples seem slow to learn. But you probably feel humble enough about your own shortcomings. Let's just be real about how we work so we can imagine how to try working another way. The world needs people who are deep. Our church and any church needs to be a people where it is OK to suffer through what we need to go through to get connected and stay there.

## We won't sink if we stop rowing long enough to pray

Maybe Peter sank because, while Jesus was in his solitary place praying, Peter was out on the lake rowing. Jesus was "going nowhere" and Peter was "getting ahead."

It would be very American to think that working hard is the only way to get somewhere, "spiritually," wouldn't it? We so believe the myth of progress! This incident on the lake is a good picture to remember when we are wondering why we aren't getting anywhere: "Why can't I do anything right? Why do I feel so weak?" — maybe all you do is row and your only option is more rowing.

*"[Jesus] went up on a mountainside by himself to pray. When evening came, he was there alone, but the boat was already a considerable distance from land, buffeted by the waves because the wind was against it." (Matthew 14:23-4)*

The wind of the world usually feels like it is against us; the waves of life often feel high. We are accustomed to rowing hard. Life is hard. We think it is normal to react by rowing *harder*, to do whatever it is we do to soothe our fears and anxieties *more*. Not Jesus. When something comes against Jesus, he prays. He thinks that is a normal reaction. It is not that Jesus isn't a tireless worker! He interrupted his retreat to feed 5000 people! It is not like he doesn't have to row hard. But even after his hard work, he stayed up into the night to pray. He didn't do his miracle gig and then say, *"I've been supernatural enough for a while; it is time to relax; let me soothe myself with a few shots."* He didn't steel himself to do his job and then collapse into his "off" personality on his own time. He was a together person living a whole life all the time. Jesus knew how to row, but he *really* knew how to pray, and it showed.

It is perilously easy to rely on more rowing rather than going deep with God. For instance, as a community, our ability to stick with Jesus has been sorely tested when it comes to buying, renting and rehabbing buildings. We have done some hard rowing when it comes to rehabbing wreckage — and we are still rowing! But even though we are great rowers; all our building issues have not been solved. I could blame the unsolved problems on stormy landlords, since they give us fits. And the waves of the Philly bureaucracy often wipe us out! It doesn't help that we are essentially in a dingy compared to the cruise-line operators who own the city. Even given all those nautical atmospherics the real problem with sinking under the load of building issues is probably more in us than in the waves.

Even though we go into a project with very few resources (money, brains, etc.), we still tend to think we should have it all together and everything should work perfectly. If it doesn't, we've been known to row harder and even yell at people who aren't keeping up! On Broad St. we worked with a general contractor who was memorably pathological, it turned out, and came with a plumber who got even with the contractor by pouring cement down the waste lines he had just put in! — it's a long story. Our building team spent sleepless nights scheming and fretting. I wouldn't say we never prayed. But I think we thought rowing harder was normal.

We tend to be like that when we're unconscious — always rowing. We have to make everything happen just right — get safe, make peace, enforce justice. How can God save us if we are always saving ourselves? How can God get a word in edgewise if we never stop talking? How can God do anything, if we have it all covered, and don't have time to listen because we're busy keeping it all covered for him? When Jesus approached the boat that time, Peter did not learn a thing until he stopped rowing and allowed for something deep with God to go on. That's why there is often a symbolic "no rowing zone" of silence in our worship. We need to stop and be with Jesus.

## We won't sink if we wait long enough to see beyond the ghosts

When something miraculous was happening, the disciples could only imagine something frightening happening. Jesus was doing the impossible; the disciples were avoiding the imponderable.

On a deep, dark, moonlit lake in the middle of the night, I'm sure they only wanted to get to solid ground, fast. But…

*During the fourth watch of the night Jesus went out to them, walking on the lake. When the disciples saw him walking on the lake, they were terrified. "It's a ghost," they said, and cried out in fear.*

*But Jesus immediately said to them: "Take courage! It is I. Don't be afraid." (Matthew 14:25-27)*

An amazing spiritual moment happens and the disciples are seeing ghosts! Seeing what we fear seems typical to me. Whenever we pray or worship or meditate, or do most anything deliberate about developing spiritually, the ghosts come up — the things that haunt us, the past sins, the insecurities about ourselves that we defend against owning and that we hide from others so they won't see them or poke at them, the things we think people are saying about us or the things they have said about us that stick with us, our fears. We would love to see God coming to us and we see a scary ghost, instead.

I remember a series of my dreams in which a monster was chasing me and I would wake up terrified. (It looked a lot like the monster in the *Alien* movies!). I told my wife about this and she wisely suggested I turn around and face the monster with God's help. I determined to do that in my next dream and I did. When the monster did not destroy me, I began to be convinced that I could face the monsters coming at me from spiritual places. Just recently, I told my spiritual director about that old dream and he questioned why the monster was wearing a baseball cap. I had never pondered that detail before! As it turns out, the ghosts-of-little-league-past, my spiritual development, my ability to love and be loved, and much more are surprisingly intertwined!

The ghosts can sink us, chase us, preoccupy us. Jesus says, "*Take courage. It is I. Don't be afraid.*" He has to keep saying that because we get so scared, we might even turn away from God! But God is on the heels of our fears. If we take a split second more to go beyond the fear, we often hear Jesus calling. That's why, when someone tells us their fearful story, we don't look at them reproachfully, we don't try to change the subject too fast, or give them some anesthesia. Instead, we bring Jesus with us into the trouble to be with them. We help each other to go deep with Jesus, not just run away from fear.

One of our friends responded to these ideas online like this: "I really resonated with this…because it is an exact description of my own spiritual walk. It's so much easier to have a surface relationship with God, where everyone sees your good deeds but your dark places are kept hidden. Whenever I find myself trying to make an effort to go deeper spiritually, I feel like I can't take the suffering and revert back to my former habits and addictions that I'm accustomed to. I still have yet to make a clean break from these things, my sins, and when I do manage to abstain for a while, then I find myself feeling guilty about a lot of less obvious sins I commit. There's always a new level of suffering and guilt to work through. If it's not intoxication and lust, then it's not loving God enough, not loving my neighbor enough, treating people poorly, judging others, or living gluttonously. My only saving grace from these things is exactly that, the saving grace from Jesus, which will be there regardless of how many times I have to go through this cycle of sin and guilt. Thanks be to God for his perfect mercy and his steadfast love.

## We won't sink if we persevere long enough to get accustomed to life outside the boat

Jesus calls his disciples to follow him. Most of them keep saying, "You don't mean follow you *there*, do you?"

Peter is not like that. He actually goes for it. Against all his better judgment, born of years in bondage to the elementary principles of the world, born of the habits of his heart and the fears that installed them, against anything that might seem remotely comfortable, he steps onto the water and enters farther into the deep things of the Spirit.

*"Lord, if it's you," Peter replied, "tell me to come to you on the water."*

*"Come," he said. Then Peter got down out of the boat, walked on the water and came toward Jesus.*

*But when he saw the wind, he was afraid and, beginning to sink, cried out, "Lord, save me!"*

*Immediately Jesus reached out his hand and caught him. "You of little faith," he said, "why did you doubt?" (Matthew 14:28-31)*

Peter got out of the boat, but he was so unaccustomed to where he was, he immediately got scared and began to sink. But even in sinking, he learned how not to sink as he called to Jesus and Jesus lifted him out.

What constitutes getting out of the boat, if that is what it takes to go deep with God? We keep learning what. It may not merely be applying principles — plenty of people have decided to actually try to walk on water and have been disappointed that the walking part of what happened to Peter isn't a universal principle. They just sink. Getting out of the boat is deeper than a controlled experiment. It is as unpredictable as Peter's relationship with Jesus out in the deep. After a few years of trying it, one thing becomes clear. Getting out one time is not enough. To keep with "things that transcend sinking" theme, the process is a bit like learning to water ski. You don't get going until you can feel how to get pulled out. Many people give up when they don't get it right off.

That was a great moment when Peter went with his deepest spiritual impulse. We are all called to get out of the boat in our own way. We'll have our moment. One of our friends stepped over the edge into motherhood recently after years of healing. One of our friends stepped over the edge into Turkey after years of dreaming about mission. One of our friends stepped over the edge into baptism after fearing the scornful reaction of her friends for many years. We'll get many opportunities. We are a church dedicated to the proposition that we are dead, and deserve to be, if we are not getting out of the boat. If the church is not moving with a deep spiritual impulse, why bother?

Jesus is holding out his hand to save each of us from what threatens to drown our relationship with God. Deep is calling, "Go deep with me." Taking that hand always feels a bit dangerous, doesn't it? Like I've been saying, there are good reasons for that.

For instance, not long ago, I watched the TV psychologist, Dr. Phil, for a minute. He had a guy and his wife on. The guy said something about his wife's bottom not being as voluptuous as when they first got married. Dr. Phil said to the man, "And what makes you think you are so great?!" The audience applauded and shouted. Everyone apparently appreciated how much shame was poured out on the stage. The wife was embarrassed about her bottom. The man quickly became embarrassed for being a jerk. (Dr. Phil was apparently not ashamed, even though he was an embarrassment to the profession of psychotherapy.) The audience reveled in someone getting exposed.

I thought, "That moment, repeated over and over, even on TV before millions of viewers, reinforces just about everything that keeps us from going deep!" And it was all in the name of trying to get at something under the surface! Shame doesn't work for good. It keeps us rowing, fearful and firmly in the boat. The best things happen when shame is forgotten in the glorious presence of God. Disciples walk on water. Husbands and wives get back together. Creatures and Creator get back together.

This part of the Jesus story ends up with the disciples forgetting their fear and shame in the presence of power and grace: *"Then those who were in the boat worshiped him, saying, 'Truly you are the Son of God.'"*

How good of God to call us out into the deep! How good of God to get in our boat with us and help us get to the other side. Relating to God is not just about getting out of the boat or not, it is taking the hand of the Son of God.

Taking his hand would be so simple, except for the emptiness, separation, loneliness, and shame we carry. We are heavily burdened and Dr. Phil tells us again, "Shape up, loser!" That's not good enough. If all we learn from Peter's lesson is to say, "I'm sure not a Peter!" That's not good enough. Circle of Hope has always been here for suffering through the loss, persevering through the work, keeping at it all through the night. We are here to be drawn into the deep where we walk with God person to person.

We have deeper places to go. We're all being called over the edge of something, just like that boat. So it is very important to maintain our safe place where we are all working on taking the hand of Jesus. We need to nurture a boat-full of cooperation — cooperating with everyone cooperating with God! Even Jesus paid attention to the fact that he was a person in a body and disciplined his body, developed his mind, and nurtured his emotions to be deep to deep with God. We're creating a place where that seems like a normal thing to do instead of just rowing against the wind, screaming about our ghosts, or sitting too paralyzed to even get out of the boat.

If we do get out, we might sink. It wouldn't be the first time. Again, that's not a very winsome slogan — *If you sink, it won't be the last time!* But sinking within a circle of hope could work out for good.

CHAPTER 6

# Doing the Word
*The Story: Jesus at Matthew's, Matthew 9*

I don't think my parents ever really understood just why little Rod made them get up and take him to Sunday school every darned week! How weird to have a devout child! What do you do, tell him to, "Stop being so religious! You're six for God's sake!?" God got to me.

When I first decided to follow Jesus as an adult (however "adult" sixteen or so might be), I was a very serious disciple — at least I was serious when my hormones and other teen things did not completely blow me away! I took a lot of what my Sunday school teachers had taught me in my childhood and thought, "I'd better put all this stuff into practice!"

One of the things they taught me still seems like a good proverb: "You might be the only Bible someone ever reads." The implication was that looking at *my life* ought to be as good as reading the Bible. I thought that sounded very important. I had enough energy to try to do it — and I *did* try to do it. I even got a reputation for being pretty much the best Bible some people had ever read!

## Scrutinous

By the time I got to college, I had the process pretty well under control. This was tested one night when I was at a party for my beloved choir director — a good man I saw every day as I sang in all his choirs learning odd, old music and enjoying singing coeds. He had shown a lot of personal interest in me and I loved him. To recognize his retirement, over a hundred of us were crammed into his house to celebrate him. At one point, someone gave a toast and passed around a literal loving cup (one with two handles and all) and we were all taking a drink in his honor. The cup got to me and I took a drink. I had tears in my eyes as I tipped the cup to him. I was really going to miss him.

I had never done anything like that. I had been sent to the Baptists for my religious training and they thought drinking was a sin — you had to say you wouldn't do it in order to "join the church!" So I had not done much (public) drinking in my day and didn't know much about it, socially. Well, come to find out, a girl I barely knew was watching me to see if the notoriously Christian guy would take a drink because she had also been taught that Christians don't drink. As far as she knew, that is what I believed, too. She was watching me to see if I was a good Bible or not!

I didn't really think taking a drink would be sinful, because I knew that the Apostle Paul prescribed wine to his disciple, Timothy, and Jesus miraculously made wine for a wedding. You can't derive a fool-proof principle of tea totaling from the Bible. But back when Christians were trying to eradicate the scourge of alcoholism that was destroying the poor, in particular (and still is), some people decided drinking was worldly and it could be done without. Looking at UPenn frat parties, and at some of the over-drinkers in our congregation, I have to admit, they had a point.

Anyway, the young woman confronted me after the party and told me I had made her "stumble" — a popular term, then, for "I don't feel good about what you did." She judged me to be a big rock blocking her path to true faith because I had, essentially, been a bad Bible.

I have been recovering from that moment ever since. It had not dawned on me that people would actually look at me *at all*, even though my Sunday school teachers had implied they would, much less that they would be so scrutinous. I had not yet felt what it was like to be under the microscope of judgmental people who seem to be basing *their* faith on whether or not *I* get it right. I can still never tell if those people are looking me over so carefully to find an excuse to not follow Jesus or if they are really afraid their whole spiritual house will fall in on them if one of us followers is not as perfect as we are cracked up to be.

## First things first

Now if I had been more astute. I would have turned to that girl and said, "Go learn what this means. Jesus says, *"You are my friends if you do what I command….This is my command: Love each other…'* (John 14:14,17). After you have mastered that, come back to me and we'll talk."

That would have been dramatic, eh? But I did not do that. And I didn't do it even though, at that point in my life, by taking a sip from that cup (by crossing the wine barrier!), I might have been feeling and showing more genuine love than I ever had in my life.

Instead of being congratulated for outdoing myself in showing honor, my acquaintance loaded on guilt because I did not meet up to her "Biblical" standards and missed the mark of holiness in her eyes. What's worse, I ended up feeling guilty about not practicing a principle that wasn't even applicable! She was not asking me to do the word, at all. Had I fulfilled her expectations I would have been observing what amounts to a pretty-good-idea that Jesus didn't even practice.

I wish I would have listened to Jesus more carefully. Then I could have done what I needed to do and responded how Jesus, the Word of God in the flesh, responds. He lived out just what James taught,

*"Do not merely listen to the word, and so deceive yourselves.*

*Do what it says.*

*Anyone who listens to the word but does not do what it says is like a person who looks at their face in a mirror and, after looking at*

◄ A CIRCLE OF HOPE

*themselves, goes away and immediately forgets what they look like."* (James 1:22-23)

Jesus didn't just <u>teach words</u> for us to hear, collect, and reorganize into theory or work into laws, Jesus <u>was the word</u>. When he looked into the word, he saw himself. Jesus did not reveal the sparkling perfection of his absolute truth; he was absolutely true in the unpredictable world of human relationships.

Likewise, we are to look into the word, into the face of Jesus, into the word of God in the Bible, into every act of the Spirit of God, and see our true selves. We need to get used to our new face and live with it, not just keep trying to put on the disguise of the "word" and appear as something we are not.

## It is always easier seen

That previous sentence was kind of thick. Rather than just sorting it into pieces and pondering the bits, let's see how Jesus was doing what James was teaching. As I help us look at one night in the Lord's life, let's not merely analyze an abstraction and the sub points about it. I hope how I lead us through the account will reflect the way the Word gave us the word: by living it, not just talking about it. Here is the story in Matthew 9:

*While Jesus was having dinner at Matthew's house, many tax collectors and "sinners" came and ate with him and his disciples. When the Pharisees saw this, they asked his disciples, "Why does your teacher eat with tax collectors and `sinners'?"*

"Why does your teacher eat with disreputable people, like Matthew?" was a good question. In Matthew's home town he was known as an unsavory character, rich with ill-gotten gain. Chances are, he had a reputation for giving wild parties. So, when Jesus came to town as the newly-famous rabbi, possible prophet and holy man, it was quite a topic for the scrutinous when he promptly decided to go to one of his alleged orgies!

You might know that when Jesus called Matthew to follow him, Matthew's job was collecting taxes for the Roman Empire. He was one of the feared collaborators. People resented him, hated him, shunned him, and since most of them were religious patriots, they thought of him as a traitor. He became an outcast. When someone is an outcast, they act like one. So Matthew's house was probably filled with the rest of the outcasts, who formed the outcast community. In that town, it was a big statement to become part of the outcasts. Maybe a couple of you remember what you went through to punk yourself out and mosh the first time, or you got a tattoo the parents forbade, or you gave all your money to the poor, or something, and it made you odd enough to feel rejected.

More likely, I suspect that most of us do not understand why being an outcast was a big deal to anyone at all. The present generation has solved the problem of rejection by pretending that being an outcast is "free" and cool and brave. We embrace it. The rap duo Outkast is a good example. They won a Grammy in 2003 for *The Whole World*. Here are some of the lyrics:

*Set a date sucka and battle we can engage,*
*I'll slice you, wife you, marry you, divorce you,*
*Throw the Porsche at u*
*is what I'm forced to do,*
*With my back against the wall,*
*crack his back y'all.*

They are just talking about a rap battle (I think), not actual violence, but it is all very kool and oukasty. We like that and give it Grammys.

In the megalopolis, lost among the millions, enslaved by huge corporations, tracked more and more by government CCTV, identified by various strings of numbers, being an "outcast" seems important. Piercing things, playing the newest music, creating an "underground" is intellectual survival, some sign of not giving in to "the man." A lot of us dress out of our thrift stores, eat vegan, refuse to work full time, create inexplicable art, or get married just to be contrary. Most of the time that is an appropriate response to the threat of being swallowed and not always merely kool.

But Matthew's town was not a megalopolis and people personally noticed and cared what side you were on. And Matthew undoubtedly cared that they cared about his profession and his friends. He cared the same way people care about whether they feel included during the little cracker time we have after our weekly meetings, when people are standing around in circles and it is hard to feel like you can get in to one if you aren't already in one. People not only did not talk to Matthew during cracker time, they made sure he knew they weren't talking to him, even though they went to elementary school together. And there is Jesus going to his house for a party!

Jesus is just doing the word. The word is, *"I came to seek and save the lost."* Extending that word, it is: *"I love you as you are. I want you back, right now. I have a way out of your self-destruction."* The word is, *"Your sin and rebellion and brokenness do not make you an outcast from God. I am God coming into your world."*

## We need a better kind of "definition" for "the word"

Matthew had already received the word from Jesus and responded by inviting him into his life and his house. So naturally he invited his friends and had a party for Jesus.

The most religious people, who told all the other Jews how it should be done, the Pharisees, were outside the courtyard gate at Matthew's. I think they were channeling the prevailing wisdom and attitudes of the day. They questioned the disciples, *"Why does your teacher eat with tax collectors and `sinners'?"* I imagine them seeing Jesus go into Matthew's house, sitting down to eat with prostitutes, drug dealers, e-mail spammers, Mark Foley, Osama bin Laden, Paris Hilton and such — and they just don't get it. The disciples aren't going in there, either, and the Pharisees are venting on them.

*"On hearing this,"* the story goes (maybe Jesus heard his disciples defending themselves against the Pharisees through the window) *"Jesus told them,"* (maybe yelled out at them) *"It is not the healthy who need a doctor, but the sick."*

This seems like obvious logic, "The sick need a doctor." But it is really quite radical. Because the assumption of most people is that the *healthy* need a doctor because the sick are infecting them! "An ounce of prevention is worth a pound of cure" — I think Ben Franklin popularized that idea right here in Philadelphia! In our town, the healthy get the doctors, and if you aren't rich or talented enough to get health insurance you get nothing. If you are in a neighborhood in which people have been kept sick for 150 years, you get a trash incinerator to make sure you have asthma. If you are mentally ill, you are sent to prison or to the streets. So Jesus is a revolutionary. The *sick* need a doctor!

You begin to see that the Word is doing the word, here, and he is not setting it out like book-learning. He is not even trying to define it properly so we can properly define our behavior and get it all right. The word that comes to us is like a story one can relate to, emulate and even continue to write. The word is the person of Jesus coming to resurrect and rule. It might help to define what that means, as one method of understanding it, as long as the definition doesn't become a heading under which Jesus is supposed to live.

## The lack of metaphorical behavior is killing me

Jesus' doctor metaphor was intended to extend, if not blow up, the categories his friends and acquaintances were working with. The Pharisees and even the disciples thought Jesus would be a spiritual doctor to protect them and inoculate their children from the disease of people like Matthew and his friends. They thought the whole society was spiritually sick and needed good, strong medicine that would drive out devils like the Romans, for sure, and then eradicate the plague of sinners that threatened to pollute the very heart of the nation and possibly kill God himself!

That's often what religious people think. For instance, I've heard it said that a few people wouldn't come to our meeting room before we got into a fixed-up one because it did not feel spiritually healthy. We met in the back room behind the check cashing store for a while; it was so dusty our rear ends were likely to be smeared with fresh gypsum dust mixed with rehab detritus. So maybe they had a point. But I've also heard that religious people, in particular, won't relate to some people in our congregation, because they are obvious sinners, and we allow sinners in the building. We've got Jews, people with suspicious sexuality, drunks, skeptics and all sorts of people hanging around who some suspect could threaten young children with their nonsense.

It is true. We have had ratty rooms and we aren't great housekeepers. And some of the people who are right at the loving heart of Circle of Hope refuse to acknowledge that Jesus is Lord. As a result, some people who see themselves as healthy or who are just barely hanging on to their spiritual health, find us dangerous. Maybe we should hand out surgical masks at the door! Because it is true, some of us *are* very dangerous, very unhealthy and infectious; and they are right where people's hearts are open to the Spirit of God; and they do not acknowledge that they are treading where people are eternally vulnerable. Some people do not acknowledge their responsibility to do the word.

But even though there was similar, legitimate danger at Matthew's house, Jesus went to the party with all those sinners and exposed himself. He turned to the people fighting outside the courtyard gate, who were probably afraid to even put a toe over the threshold because they were so obsessed with their own health and safety that they didn't even know they weren't concerned for others — and he said to them: *"Go and learn what this means: `I desire mercy, not sacrifice.'* (Hosea 6) *For I have not come to call the righteous, but sinners."*

You don't have to spend six years getting a doctorate in theology to get the word. Jesus takes three minutes to put it together for them and for us. He tells it with his mouth and with his actions.

## Doing the word means giving and receiving mercy

The heart of the word is getting over the threshold and going to Matthew's. Generally, that means the word says, *"The whole world is a Matthew's house and God loves everyone in it."* Specifically, that means, *"When I invite Jesus to my house, He'll come, just like he came to Matthew's."*

That might sound simple, but I don't think we should be surprised if we are as frustrated as the Pharisees and as confused as the disciples about what the Word means. We tend to argue with God about it all the time. I've had many people ask me, "Why would God want to come to *my* house — what's in it for him?"

It's not that people don't want to have a relationship with God. They definitely want God "in the house." They are just so hurt, so defensive, so angry and so accustomed to seeing things their own way that they can't believe anyone will relate to them mercifully. They are thinking, *"I wouldn't join a club that would have me for a member"* all the time. To have God be so interested in them makes them suspicious. Doesn't he have better things to do? But we need to see who's at the door. Hearing that word of mercy and receiving it is the first step to expressing it.

## Doing the word means giving up the daily battle to be right

The heart of the word is getting over what is ruined and going with what Jesus brings. Generally that means the word says, *"Jesus is restoring Creation, starting here and now."* Specifically, that means, *"It is not my job to bring the world around right by my careful behavior. My self-centered sense of the value of my sacrifice is destructive."* In other words, "When I see Jesus breaking my rules, I need to learn something new."

Maybe that sounds odd, since even non-Christians seem to think that Jesus is all about being righter than everyone else. Plus, Christians seem to be all about waving their Spirit-inspired book to prove how right we are, "Right here on page 567!" We hardly feel good unless we go through the day fighting for what makes us feel better in relation to everyone who is making us feel bad. So many of us feel so bad, so dissatisfied, or so skeptical most of the time, that we are always trying to get some piece of wisdom or knowledge that will make us feel good, satisfied and peaceful. And we are constantly irritated by those who are keeping it from us.

This tendency to feel like what is happening *is just not right enough* is easy to see in married couples or in couples who have sex but don't call themselves married. The spiritual intimacy of sex brings up a whole host of inner needs for everyone whose spiritual sensors aren't totally numbed. As a result, one's mate can regularly seem so *not all right!* They are always doing something wrong or not responding to what is obvious. We can end up in a constant struggle to get something. We seem to feel, "If I ever forgive, or let go of the struggle, or become satisfied with less than the best I deserve, I might lose my chance for happiness!"

Without God in the world, those losses are intolerable. But God has come to Matthew's house and that is exactly the kind of house each of us is. We have been shown mercy. Mercy is knocking at our hearts. To do the word, we must start by opening up to the reality that the Word makes us right by doing the word. We don't get the mercy by getting the word right.

The Word is about how God is living in relationship with us. Likewise, for us, receiving the word is about living in love, too. What our bodies do, not just what our minds think is right, makes the difference. I like the way Eugene Peterson says it in **The Jesus Way**: *"We can't suppress the Jesus way in order to sell the Jesus truth. The Jesus way and the Jesus truth must be congruent. Only when the Jesus way is organically joined with the Jesus truth do we get the Jesus life."*

## Doing the word means training our lives for mercy

The heart of the word is accepting a new kind of definition. The heart of the definition is mercy. Generally, that means we can hear God say, *"When you see me dying with the sins of the world on my shoulders, erasing the gap between God and humankind, and upending the powers, you will see the epitome of mercy, if you have eyes to see."* Specifically, that means, *"If I want to be right with God,*

*I need to live like Jesus. When I see Jesus going where I haven't been, I need to follow — even to Matthew's."*

We *really* argue with God about the call to connect with people who need mercy all evening! The disciples must have been thinking, like I think we do, *"If you go into that house, Jesus, what's in it for you? You'll be contaminated by those people. They are so obviously messed up that the life will be sucked out of you!"*

Jesus turns to us and says, *"The word is mercy, not sacrifice."* By extension that is: "I am not sacrificing, as if I were making some kind of deal or working magic. I am living. This is living. The alternative to this is dying. The alternative to having a life of mercy is sucking the life out of others, out of the whole planet and still needing more, until you train yourself to be one big black hole."

At least I think he says something like that. I wish I could remember to say things like that with sincerity and integrity. So often I am flabbergasted by some scrutinous person and thrown into a defensive fit of guilt and shame, as if I didn't know the Word or the word or any words at all!

I want my convictions to be accessible when I am wrapped up in trying to follow Jesus into mercy. There was a time when we had a series of heroin addicts living with us (it was an era when Dad might bring one to dinner any day!). We just couldn't stand the thought that one of our friends would be out on the street. Even though we felt mercy, it was still hard to tolerate how our friends did not abide by the family rules, or even the rules of hygiene, much less did they relate lovingly and respond instantly to our mercy by shaping up! (Well, one is still clean and functioning; but another OD'd and died in an alley). I need to hold on to the word and not revert to applying principles that are easier for me to control and more effective for judging others wrong. Mercy brings its own reward in God's time. I can't expect to control the results with my good behavior.

That's hard.

I've kind of given up jumping through the hoops of unmerciful people and I'm trying to give up jumping through the hoops of my own sense of what's right. No doubt someone will read this and think I am just trying to get away with something because I secretly want to go out with Matthew and sink into some kind of depravity. Maybe my words imply that. So I'll leave that up to the Holy Spirit and my track record to convince you that all I am really struggling with is doing the word. I'm the one who wanted to be the sixteen-year-old Bible, after all!

CHAPTER 7

# Generating Justice and Hope in Our Neighborhood
*The Story: Jesus tells the story of the merciful Samaritan, Luke 10*

In *Wanted* (2008), James McAvoy plays an anxious, cubicled loser who discovers that his lost father is a super-trained assassin taking orders from Morgan Freeman to kill people. Things go very wrong after McAvoy realizes he has his own set of genetic gifts. They go so wrong that Angelina Jolie is forced to kill everyone. I did not spoil a thing for you by revealing the limited plot — some guilty pleasures are not about plot. Beneath the thin surface of this movie is the longing of all the abused and enslaved people of the postmodern era to become someone and to give themselves to a larger cause. Kneaded into that gooey frustration is the despair of the young, who are not surprised when St. Morgan Freeman is revealed to be another leader who thwarts one's idealism.

In a deteriorating world, it is hard to know just how much to keep trying. We don't always know what to do with ourselves, but we would like to know. This confusion applies to Christians, too, especially American ones, who have been force-fed a brand of theology that convinced us that we are souls to save, spirits waiting to be released from the doomed planet, which will soon go up in smoke at Armageddon (pause to consider another movie in the *Wanted* genre, only Ben Affleck gets a chance to be someone).

While we are waiting to "go to heaven" we can be a little muddled, looking around for our personal destiny to be realized in a doomed world. For instance, one of my friends doesn't want to become too cubicled, so he makes sure he keeps one night a week at his bartending job — that feels real to him. Another friend tattooed parts of his body that could not be hidden under long sleeves to make sure he would always be something other than what he is supposed to be. I can understand these impulses, but I think there is a better alternative.

N.T. Wright complains about the teachers who planted our despair and offers an important reframe in *Surprised by Hope*. He says, "To suppose that we are saved, as it were, for our own private benefit, for the restoration of our own relationship with God (vital though that is!) and for our eventual homecoming and peace in heaven (misleading though that is!) is like a boy being given a baseball bat as a present and insisting that since it belongs to him, he must always and only play with it in private. But of course you can only do what you're meant to do with a baseball bat when you're playing with other people. And salvation only does what it is meant to do when those who have been saved, are being saved, and will one day fully be saved realize that they are saved not as souls but as wholes and not for themselves alone but for what God now longs to do through them"

As a church, we are trying to figure out what we can best do with the talents being revealed and the new bat we have been given. Sharing, as we now do, the resurrection life of Jesus, released from our slavery (even cubicle slavery), we are trying to get on with what God longs to do through us. Isaiah 59:9-12 pretty much summarizes where we want to go:

*"If you do away with the yoke of oppression, with the pointing finger and malicious talk, and if you spend yourselves in behalf of the hungry and satisfy the needs of the oppressed, then your light will rise in the darkness, and your night will become like the noonday. The LORD will guide you always; he will satisfy your needs in a sun-scorched land and will strengthen your frame. You will be like*

## GENERATING JUSTICE AND HOPE IN OUR NEIGHBORHOOD

*a well-watered garden, like a spring whose waters never fail. Your people will rebuild the ancient ruins and will raise up the age-old foundations; you will be called Repairer of Broken Walls, Restorer of Streets with Dwellings."*

We're spending ourselves, receiving guidance, building a well-watered garden, rebuilding the walls and streets of the dark and sun-scorched land of Philadelphia. Generating justice and hope in our neighborhood is fundamental to showing the resurrection that happened and that will happen. We're into exercising reckless love as best we can be.

When Circle of Hope was just a good idea and not yet an amazing community of Jesus followers, the founders decided that we needed to rely on more than individual good will to keep us generating. They imagined an agency that would keep us focused outside ourselves and on the needs of others, both in our fair city and around the world. It will always be bogus to say we are moving along with Jesus if we aren't interested in healing, helping, doing good, and demanding justice — because that is what Jesus is moving along doing himself. So after a few years of trial and error we came up with Circle Venture. We managed to get the Mennonite Central Committee to fund a director. Then the Circle Venture Team came up with the idea of encouraging people to create Mission Teams to lead us. Each team launches from the genius of a small, focused group that shares a passion. I love what we have done and what we are doing and what we just might do this next year to show compassion and share God's love in practical ways! People aren't going to get to know the Jesus I know unless we are out and about doing good.

And we *are* doing good! (Not just us, of course, Christians are pouring out love all over the planet). As this is being written, we just opened another Thrift Store that loves customers and generates funds for loving the poor and oppressed worldwide; we are working on a "carbon neutral" step of handing out free CFL light bulbs to our neighbors — something like environmental evangelism, and we are blessing a group that is forming Shalom House for proactive peacemaking. Mission Teams spring up and die off according to our inspiration, but the rising and dying and rising is all about generating compassion.

## But, of course, we are still tempted to justify our self-centeredness

We were absolutely right to think that if we did not have an agency of some kind pushing us and reminding us, we would not be able to face everything that requires our love. The problems calling for compassion and the needs calling for service are huge, difficult and daunting. Philly is competing to be the murder capital of the nation! Poverty and injustice have created people acclimated to them — like our neighbors who use the check cashing store below one of our sites. Our streets are a home for the homeless and mentally ill — they congregate at the St. Francis Inn, a few blocks from another site. Our government and private agencies that protect children are broken, as well as our schools — ask our social workers and teachers! And that doesn't even take us to the city limits! Then we start talking about slavery in Saudi Arabia, cyclones in Bangladesh and deforestation in the Amazon. Something needs to push us to keep growing hearts big enough to look at all that!

The challenges all around us are so big they make us hesitant to get engaged, but an even greater inhibition to expressing compassion is what's been built into us. We're too much like the people Jesus warned about, *"They clean the outside of the cup and dish, but inside they are full of greed and self-indulgence"* (Matthew 23). It is what's inside us that is the greater inhibition to sharing God's love in practical ways. We have all been cultured by what is probably the most narcissistic society ever. (I don't have data to compare previous sinners with us, so you decide). Without God fighting for us, there is almost nothing forming us that encourages us to think of someone else for more than a few minutes, so we have trouble doing that. Circle of Hope can even resent Circle Venture for making us think of others for the few minutes we allow it to do that — and we created it to do that!

# GENERATING JUSTICE AND HOPE IN OUR NEIGHBORHOOD

The hope streaming through this chapter is that we will manage to see beyond ourselves and follow Jesus in a life of compassion, regardless of what's outside and in. And I think we are we're doing that, even though it is never easy. It is hard for us and it was hard for people in Jesus' day. One of the most famous parables Jesus gave us, "The Good Samaritan," was given in response to a man who was stuck on himself. A man came to Jesus with a question, and seemed to think he was "all that" — he was having trouble seeing outside of the image he had of himself. In general (as a society and as a generation) we are strikingly bent like this man. As similar people, determined to generate compassion in our neighborhoods, it will help to spend some time listening to Jesus again as he talks to him:

"On one occasion an expert in the law stood up to test Jesus. 'Teacher,' he asked, 'what must I do to inherit eternal life?'

"What is written in the Law?" [Jesus] replied. "How do you read it?"

*He answered: "'Love the Lord your God with all your heart and with all your soul and with all your strength and with all your mind" (Deut. 6:5); and, `Love your neighbor as yourself.'"(Lev. 19:18)*

"You have answered correctly," Jesus replied. "Do this and you will live."

But **he wanted to justify himself,** so he asked Jesus, 'And who is my neighbor?'" (Luke 10:25ff)

Like many Americans, the man who tested Jesus was very religious. 75-80% of the USonians will tell a pollster we are Christians. Jesus congratulates the man on being so correct. Then he tells him, "Now live correctly."

<u>But the man wanted to justify himself.</u> He wants to make sure he is getting it right. He wants to make sure he can tell himself that he doesn't need to do anything more to inherit eternal life, that he has the bases covered. So he asks for more definition, just to be sure: "Who is my neighbor?" He seems to be calculating, "Have I gotten to all of my neighbors? What is the minimum number of neighbors I must love to be OK with God? How much do I have to do to get an 'A'?"

"So just who is my neighbor?" is a very *narcissistic* question, among other things — a question that is all about *me* and *my image*. It is an outside of the cup and not an inside of the cup question. It is at least ironic that the man is preoccupied with what neighboring means to *him!* — when neighboring, by definition, has to do with *someone else!* One of the biggest temptations of our era is to be that self-absorbed — so wrapped up in our "lifestyle," so protective of our "way of life," that we think twice before sharing even the leavings of our table.

## We Tend to Be Like Narcissus

You remember Narcissus. In the Greek myth he was the son of the river god Cephissus. He was about the most perfectly formed youth, ever. The mountain nymph, Echo, fell in love with him at first sight, but Narcissus was cold to her. She pined away for him until she became just a lonely voice. This disturbed the god Nemesis so much that he caused Narcissus to go drink from a particular pool where he would see his reflection. Narcissus was so entranced by his beautiful image that he could not tear himself away. He withered by the pool until he became planted by it, a narcissus flower. Some versions say he fell in love with himself when he looked in the pool and, unable to find consolation, died of sorrow. Some say he fell in and drowned. Painters have always loved him, too — perfect youth that he was.

Psychologists latched on to this myth to name people who are unhealthily obsessed with how they present themselves. The name helps the doctors describe people who have so much interest in their image that they have withered away inside. They are so outward they can't connect with the inward.

Isn't that like the man Jesus met? His immediate response to the call to "love your neighbor as yourself" sounds like a retort I often hear when a venture of compassion is brought up: "Who is *my* neighbor? How does this apply to *me*? When will I know I have served my neighbor most effectively, so I don't waste *my time* or *my money*? How do I go *get the best experience* of serving my neighbor? — I have an hour on Thursdays."

When the Reconciliation Team brings up racism, some person almost always says, "I didn't have slaves. My ancestors didn't do anything. Why should I feel guilty or do anything?" Justice means *just us* for a lot of us. When the Water Team brings up Darfur, someone asks, "Why is it my responsibility to worry about their water? We have problems right here in Philly!" When the Circle of Peacemakers talks about proactive peacemaking someone will say, "We solved our issues, they'll just have to solve theirs." If there were an oldies radio show playing the top ten American Christian attitudes, they would all begin with do-re-ME.

## It is "radical" to be anything else but into ourselves

We can hardly imagine another way to think than to think about ourselves first. So Jesus tells a story about a radical to help us get the idea. Jesus is a radical telling a story about another radical like himself. And he is telling the story to a particular man and to a group of people who don't get what the story means; they don't understand the heart of what matters.

Most people think "radical" means *wild* or *extreme*. But radicals only look wild because they are different; they aren't tamed by the powers that be. A radical is just *basic* — like the radical, or root, of a number. They are people who are single-minded, simple in their assessment of what is important. You could be a radical Phillies fan or a radical Shiite. If you are a radical Christian, you are single-minded about Jesus, and about loving God and others. *Radical* and *Christian* should always go together, I think. As Paul would put it, we've taken off our old, sullied-up self and put on the one Jesus has delivered, which is being restored in the image of its creator (Col. 3:10). When Jesus says: *"If your eyes are good, your whole body will be full of light,"* I think he uses "good" in the sense of simple, singular, unalloyed. His followers focus the way he does. They are radicals, like him. Calling someone a non-radical Christian would be an oxymoron.

Jesus is focused when he tells the story. He is having one of those moments that must seem painfully redundant to him as he talks to someone who thinks they present so well that they can debate the fine points of being good with God. Maybe that is why his replies often get so colorful, *"You are like whitewashed tombs, which look beautiful on the outside but on the inside are full of dead men's bones and everything unclean. In the same way, on the outside you appear to people as righteous but on the inside you are full of hypocrisy and wickedness."* (Matthew 23 again)

I'm sure he would be comforted if he could merely offer a colorful metaphor or tell a good parable and everyone would instantly be eager to follow him in his way. Instead, he is often bouncing his truth off narcissists. [See Christopher Lasch, *The Culture of Narcissism*, if you're really into the sociology]

<u>In our day, it is even "radical" to consider someone else to be as real as we are</u>

Messiah College drafted me to teach their course on Urban Theology to undergrads one year. I hardly ever got a discussion going about theology — which says a lot about my teaching skills! The lack of engagement also said a lot about where the students were coming from. Most of them were decidedly not urban and were equally untheological. I couldn't get a discussion about urban challenges or about God going, but the students could get a lot of discussion going about a few of their feelings, "Why do I have to take *theology*? What does this have to do with *me*? How will *I* ever *use* this?" I don't think the lack of interest was merely about the students being 19 or merely about me being incompetent; it was about them being a product of their society. If they could not immediately consume or understand the value of my teaching, it was not real. Both urban people and God were not there, so they had trouble seeing either as relevant.

Being trained by the same society might make it hard to hear the message of Jesus' story. If people are not like us, or with us, or useful to us, they are not real.

<u>In our day, it is "radical" to look out for someone else's best interests</u>

This may not be true about everyone, but a lot of us are constantly making a deal to get the best we can for ourselves, and hopefully, to keep trading up. We have taken the pursuit of excellence way over the top —
not just *healthy* bodies, *ripped* bodies,
not just an *adequate* place to live, *gigantic* houses;
not just *jobs* that pay the bills and contribute to the community, *careers* that match our full potential and dreams,
not just *partners* that we love and serve, but *soulmates* who satisfy all our fantasies,
not just *intimacy* that matches our spiritual and relational development, but *supercharged capacities* created by pills and surgery that amplify our erogenous zones;
not just *good times* of self-expression and friendship, but the *best of everything*, the most exotic dishes of food, the wildest vacations that no one else has had.
We're trained to compete for the best and the most, and we consider a life of aggressive consuming to be self-development. We tend to worship the people who get it all. Caring about what others get is irrelevant, or even a detraction from meeting our goals — unless, of course, one's goal is to get a reputation as the best care-giver, ever, and to put that on a resume! Trying to look out for the interests of others goes against some deeply ingrained habits.

<u>In our day it is "radical" to act outside our personal worlds</u>

For a lot of people, this could be how the day often goes: I go from my private bedroom to my own car to my own office, then back to my single family dwelling with my own master suite, complete with my private bathroom; then I go to the store, with my headphones on to protect my space, where I am provided an endless array of personal choices, many of which are packaged as single servings. We never have to leave our privacy. The ability to do our own thing is practically our definition of human rights!

Robert Bellah tells a story about a man who grew up in a broken home and ended up drifting into a life that was focused on the pursuit of his private pleasures — drugs and sex, mainly. His life was all about what he wanted. Later the man got married and settled down. He had three kids and worked like crazy to fulfill the family's needs and his own sense of self-development as a successful man. His 60-70 hour work week finally destroyed his marriage. He was shocked by his failure so he decided to change. He got married again and this time when something needed to be sacrificed, it was the job. His family became the place where he found his "meaning." Upon first glance, the man's story seems to develop into some kind of conversion, until one realizes that in each phase of his life, he was still the same kid doing his own thing for his own satisfaction. Even when his goal was to be a great family man, it was still all about him finding meaning. Pleasures, job success, perfect family — he still never connected his actions to anything but his personal preference or performance in the comfort of his own little world.

Trying to react with compassion, when we are taught not to share, or even connect, pits us against some powerful forces.

## So I Miss the Forest for My Trees

The man who tested Jesus had such a self-centered reaction, it was destroying any chance for him to care for someone but himself. It was like he was walking through a forest on the most beautiful evening of the summer — sunset, flowers, birds, everything, but he didn't notice the scenery because he was obsessed with what was going on *with him*. We're so likely to be like that! We're talking to Jesus, or trying to listen to someone talk about Jesus, or considering what expression we could make of the love of Jesus — walking through beautiful forest of the Lord. But what we are thinking about is, "My latest infatuation left me," or "My fat is traumatizing me," or "My failures make me look inadequate," or "The pollen is making my eyes swell." If you aren't smarting from the accusation too much to hear it some more — we tend to see only ourselves.

Translate that society-affirmed self-absorption into walking through the everyday world and the results are devastating. People could need us and we wouldn't even see them; they might not penetrate our zone of personal obsession. How could we really care? How could we love our neighbors as ourselves unless they loved us for ourselves first, or at least loved us back? What would be in it for us?

The funny thing is, when we hear this story of the merciful Samaritan, we often react to it in such a self-referential way. We hear about these bad guys who didn't help a suffering man, and we hear about the Samaritan guy who did help, and we get all upset about ourselves — *"Did I stop for enough hitchhikers or people with flat tires? Should I have given that panhandler money? Do I have a reputation for being a good Sam?"* And there we go again, all obsessed with being justified or not.

## There are a lot of changes to make before compassionate service seems likely

People who generate compassionate service don't share love in practical ways merely so they can get a spiritual rush or have a better spiritual resume or have an experience they can make a speech about, or just because they have enough money to do something good (even though rushes and reputations and generosity may result when ones shares). Compassionate people are through with "it's all about me" — the headphones are off and they are hearing God. They are part of a community with a purpose — not living in a walled compound protecting "theirs." They are moved with the world's plight and have something to contribute — they are beyond themselves with love — just like the person in the Lord's story:

### A CIRCLE OF HOPE

*Jesus said: "A man was going down from Jerusalem to Jericho, when he fell into the hands of robbers. They stripped him of his clothes, beat him and went away, leaving him half dead. A priest happened to be going down the same road, and when he saw the man, he passed by on the other side. So too, a Levite, when he came to the place and saw him, passed by on the other side. But a Samaritan, as he traveled, came where the man was; and when he saw him, he took pity on him. He went to him and bandaged his wounds, pouring on oil and wine. Then he put the man on his own donkey, took him to an inn and took care of him. The next day he took out two silver coins and gave them to the innkeeper. `Look after him,' he said, `and when I return, I will reimburse you for any extra expense you may have.'*

*"Which of these three do you think was a neighbor to the man who fell into the hands of robbers?"*

*The expert in the law replied, "The one who had mercy on him."*

*Jesus told him, "Go and do likewise." (Luke 10:30-37)*

There are three things, here, that we narcissistic types tend to miss. Let me point them out and leave it at that so we can go and do likewise:

<u>The story is about the basic miracle of history.</u>

The story is told by God who is coming to despised victims, like us, who are, essentially, lying by the side of the road. At his own expense God saved us when we were unconscious, after we had been beaten up by the robbers who tried to steal our lives. If you are chained to a cubicle, or whatever, right now; God is not overlooking you.

The story is not just about you or me as if one of us were God in the story. That's where we usually place ourselves — as the Good Samaritan, or not — as the star of the story. The story is *first* about you and me as if we were the robbed one. Once God rescues us, we can start thinking about finding the others who have been robbed. But even then, it will always be a miracle that anyone is rescued at all.

<u>The story is about community.</u>

Jesus is telling this story to form a people who are committed to generating compassion. It is told to create a power for justice in the world that can stand against the antichrist powers that be, a power for reform, and a power to bring redemption.

So often we read the stories of Jesus as if he were writing a book and he thought we would read it in the privacy of our carrel at the library. But what he is really doing is traveling with a band of disciples and teaching everything in public so everyone can mull over what he's saying — together. The story is told to create a culture, to shape a people. Jesus presumes neighborhood. If we don't live in that context, how can we hear what he is saying at all? Compassion is the culture of our community, not just an individual act we personally express or experience periodically.

<u>The story is about societal change.</u>

Jesus is addressing a teacher of the law, a respected and even powerful individual in his society. He is doing it as something of an outcast, a beggar, a person totally reliant on what he says and does for respect. Jesus has no given position in the power structure at all.

What's more, he is telling a story about a person who is an even greater outcast from the Jewish establishment than himself, a Samaritan, who is doing what a priest and a Levite would not do for their very good personal reasons. Priests had high rank in temple worship; Levites were like priest aides, and very respected. Both are apparently on their way to worship in Jerusalem, but they are too busy to stop and worship by the side of the road. True worship would have been serving the man in the ditch (check out Matthew 25).

By addressing this very pointed story to a respected person, Jesus is doing more than just saying, *"You need to change your mind and ways, man!"* He is also saying *"The whole society needs to act like this merciful Samaritan. I am speaking this to the powers that be: oppressing Samaritans is wrong; ignoring the weak by the side of the road is wrong. I'm not just talking to you, personally, but to all of you."* And to us, too.

We often don't do a thing because we think it is all about "me" and we don't have much to do with "us." For instance, here is a random list of things, specific to *us*, that are easy for us to miss:

- Most of us totally surrendered to the narcissistic war against Iraq. We bought the argument that it was logical to remake a country to be like our country for the sake of our own national interests. But if democracy means anything, the Christians certainly have the right to tell the government to be like the good Samaritan and stop justifying yourself!
- We let our local governments zone entire municipalities off from each other. Lower Merion might prefer a wall down City Ave! Shouldn't the question be, "Who is your neighbor Philadelphia? Isn't it the "edge city" of King of Prussia?" Wouldn't Jesus tell a story that would teach us to share?
- We tend not to blink when a new government policy encourages more narcissism. When U.S. manufacturers sell cars with higher fuel economy standards in Europe but resist congressional demands for quicker compliance with higher levels here, isn't the question, "Who is your neighbor, U.S.A.?" What's more, isn't the question, "How many people have your policies left lying by the side of the road?"
- Personally, it is very hard to discipline our schedules to get deliberate compassion into them. The best we can do is not run over people who cross against the light, or give some of our disposable income to the church, or go "that one time" we went to help Katrina victims. In Christ, we are neighbors to all we meet.

## We will keep practicing

When Jesus tells his story, he knows he is the king. He knows he will soon be left by the side of the road, robbed of his life, and the powers that be will pass him by, along with his friends. But some Samaritan with eyes to see him and not just himself will lay him in the place from which he will rise again. It is a miracle story. The compassion that leads Jesus to the cross is the key to undermining the forces death and destruction that are killing creation. A compassion that would die in order to love is the seed of the kingdom.

Jesus thinks his story is very practical. The parable isn't just about each of us and how God is trying to wheedle his way into our private worlds and get us to do things that have no immediate pay-off but which ought to be done, anyway. It certainly is not about how he wants to make it impossible for us to get ahead and wants to steal away our freedom to get what we want. The story is about God and what God does, and what happens as a result. No wonder he says, "If you have ears to hear, hear!" We're so often on a continuous loop. We're in danger of becoming lovely flowers living by the pools of our self-image, incapacitated by our self-centeredness.

Let me leave you with one last story about someone who had ears to hear. When we first had a meeting place on Tenth and Locust, we carved out the tiniest counseling office ever seen to house the beginnings of Circle Counseling. We had people with skills and we were making friends who needed psychological care, but our new friends could not afford the cost of care. Our Director started providing counseling herself in her "spare time" and then started engaging psychologists and psychiatrists to give some hours for low fees and even for free. It has been a constant place of healing, behind the scenes, for years. Periodically, one of our leaders will tell us how they were released to deeper faith by the help they gained from the therapist. Now Circle Counseling has its own building, five therapists and a new vision for expanded care. Every healing is moving from death to life and a sure sign that the resurrection is coming — and is even here. It is another way to generate compassion in the neighborhood.

We're hardly languishing by the pool looking at ourselves or looking at someone looking at themselves. Circle Venture is a tool in God's hands to make sure we never do.

CHAPTER 8

# Building Community as a Living Organism
*The Story: Jesus and the Sons of Thunder, Matthew 20*

For a lot of people, Christianity would be a lot better if it didn't include relating to all those Christians! St. John of the Cross (1542-1591) wrote his famous prose-poem *The Dark Night of the Soul* when he was imprisoned by *fellow believers* in the Carmelite Order for trying to reform them. They lashed him weekly. He was kind of eccentric, to be sure, but one would not expect your "brothers" to beat you, no matter how off-center! He must have thought, "Now *that* is not what I expected when I committed my life to the order!"

It is hard to say whether John's deep connection with God got him into trouble or his trouble deepened his connection with God. I picture him in his cell, in which he could barely turn around, reciting his forbidden paraphrase of the Song of Songs in beautiful Spanish. The dove of peace comes to him:

*She lived in solitude,*
*and now in solitude has built her nest;*
*and in solitude he guides her,*
*he alone, who also bears*
*in solitude the wound of love.*

It would be wonderful if abuse from our loved ones reduced us to love and made us like the Lover who bore all wounds so completely. What it often does, however, is confirm our suspicions and send us trotting toward the door.

Some of our wounds of love are very deep, and we did not take them on voluntarily. They often make us very leery of making new relationships, even though we desire the connections so much. If you're 25-40, especially, you grew up in a particularly disjointed era. The incident of divorce was higher and became "normal." Your friends created alternative ways to connect, mostly as free agents who didn't enter into marriage or other commitments too readily. Thus we had Chandler, Monica and the rest of the "Friends" representing how nice a little untraditional tribe could be (1994-2004) and "Seinfeld" representing how weird it could be (1989-1998).

More than one of my friends has sat in the meetings of the church for years considering whether they can get over their wounds of love, deal with all these people and make the leap into identifying with an even odder "tribe." The church is not like a beer commercial where an affinity for the team and Bud holds everyone together — somehow *that* seems normal. In the church, *Jesus* brings together a motley crew (that often looks like Motley Crue around here) and expects them to share the love that intimacy with God engenders. One friend came to the meeting for months and carefully left before it was over each week lest she be forced to talk to someone. I first got to know her by chasing after her down the stairs (which was pretty scary for her!). It was a big step the night she went and got a cookie. It took over a year for her to venture into a cell group, but then she wouldn't say anything. Now she hosts one in her home. But trust has been hard to give and receive.

## We expect community in Christ to be difficult to understand and practice

Someone discovered recently that Circle of Hope actually has a rather elaborate *plan* for how we build community as a "cell church." They were amazed! They were impressed! — so unexpectedly organized! They had no idea there was a secret plan — or anything planned at all!

## BUILDING COMMUNITY AS A LIVING ORGANISM

If the Cell Plan is a secret plan, it isn't a very good secret. We publicly train people in it relentlessly. The "secret wisdom" of Circle of Hope is online if you like things written down.

In one of the trainings for the Cell Plan, someone saw one paragraph in the side column of our little book, and thought we might be a little unusual, for Christians. They didn't want to say anything in the group, so they sidled up to me during the break and said, "I was thumbing through the book as you were talking and I saw a heading on one of the pages, I don't know where now, but it said 'Orgasm.' Why in the world does the cell plan talk about that?"

"No, no," I said. It says <u>organism</u>, like a living being, like cells that make up organs which are the basic building blocks of living things, like bodies. We're an organism!" I don't know if that means we have orgasms, but that is not what the book is specifically about.

This is what they hadn't read in the Cell Plan yet: *"An organism has a life. An organization is a concept waiting to be filled with life. We aren't waiting, we aren't merely prospective, we aren't laboring under the condemnation of some structure to which we need to conform; we exist as who we are. We are being built by God; we feed on the Spirit and develop."* I hope that kind of feels like an orgasm to someone, but that's not immediately what we're looking to produce. What we *are* looking forward to is functioning like a body, or we are not much of the Church, at all.

When Paul was talking about how God put us together as his family, one of his favorite metaphors was the human body…

*"The body is a unit, though it is made up of many parts …. So it is with Christ. For we were all baptized by one Spirit into one body—whether Jews or Greeks, slave or free—and we were all given the one Spirit to drink. Now the body is not made up of one part but of many….God has arranged the parts in the body, every one of them, just as he wanted them to be."* (1 Corinthians 12:12-14)

What he is saying is more than a metaphor, of course. Paul artfully describes a spiritual reality. Becoming the body of Christ comes from "drinking" a common Spirit — the creative, redemptive

Spirit of God, who is forming new persons and uniting them into a new body that is the incarnation of Jesus in the world. We are that body — at least a part of it.

If you have talked to Christians in the United States very much, you know that, by and large, the only way they have to explain how one is a Christian is to say, "I go to church." Some might say, "I go to Circle of Hope." They rarely say something like Paul might say, like, *"I am a member of the body of Christ. Some of us meet together on Sundays on Broad Street, and over on Frankford Ave., and all over the region in cells all week."* Somehow, a lot of us got it in our heads that church is a *thing* and the only body they could talk much about is their own. So their body goes to church. They are never really part of a "we;" they visit the "we."

Maybe this doesn't surprise you. After all, we all seem to have a perverse instinct for aloneness. We get more isolated all the time. Like I said before, we sometimes label the disconnection "freedom." The *economy*, which is the only togetherness we feel safe to talk about, as a nation, runs on everyone's lifetime goal to fill the vast emptiness we feel inside with the stuff and experiences that get inserted in the places that love can't seem to stick. We run on the perverse instinct, born of experience and honed by the philosophy of the day, that we are alone, and we form habits that we don't even know are a result of running on our instincts. As a result, one of the things we are not very good at is being an organism called the body of Christ, even when we want to be one. To be such an organism requires the new spiritual instinct born of being one with God through Jesus Christ.

## We're working with Jesus on being a body

We want to freely live out of our new Spirit-installed instinct to form an organism building community. We want to be alive in the Spirit. We want to be much more than a religious "shop," or just a means to personal fulfillment, or merely another organization. We trying to listen as Jesus teaches us, just like he taught the first circle he formed, about how to be a "we." What he said about that one day got recorded as a prescriptive memory. Here's the story:

As Jesus continued his public ministry he attracted a number of people who left their normal routine and traveled with him. He called some of these people to be in his inner circle, his leadership team. We call them the twelve disciples. But many others came alongside to be his people, too. Some women of means, in particular, apparently bankrolled the operation. Jesus and his crew were like an amoeba which grows by enveloping and including more material and nutrients. People not only heard what he said, they saw what he did and experienced his presence. The life Jesus brought fed them and connected them and shaped them, day by day, as much as their remembrance of his teaching shaped them later. More and more people were included in this new people that formed around Jesus. There is little doubt that Jesus meant to be the king of that kingdom and let us see what he was talking about.

One of the women who traveled with Jesus was Salome, the wife of Zebedee the fisherman. She was apparently Jesus' aunt (although the record isn't totally clear on that). Jesus had called his cousins right off their fishing boat one day and they followed him into his ministry. Their mother followed her boys. On this day,

"The mother of Zebedee's sons came to Jesus with her sons and, kneeling down, asked a favor of him. 'What is it you want?' he asked.

She said, 'Grant that one of these two sons of mine may sit at your right and the other at your left in your kingdom.'"

I'm not sure if experiencing this scene made Jesus gulp, or not. Salome was in the dirt, her boys were looking on expectantly. She was asking for glory at Jesus' right and left hand. She wanted the ultimate promotion for her Sons of Thunder, as they were nicknamed. "Make them 1st Vice Presidents when you get to be CEO!" She apparently hadn't understood much about how he was teaching them all to live, yet. And she hadn't observed too much about how he was living!

Jesus had just been prophesying his humiliating death at the hands of the Romans and *his* heart was set on Jerusalem and what awaited him there. But this mother's heart was set on honor and ease for her sons — and maybe a little fame for herself as the mother of such fine sons! Salome and her sons had a lot of faith —they were sure that Jesus would come into his own as the leader of a great kingdom. But they didn't see how that could happen in any way but the way they imagined — even when Jesus told them how it would happen! You've got to admire such ambition! But it all boiled down to self-seeking.

This instinctual behavior, this self-seeking, blocks people from having a right relationship with God. You can see it messing up Salome and Jesus. It not only messes up our relationship with God, it also blocks us from having good relationships with others. And we'll see the bad relationships happen when the other disciples get wind of James and John trying to score first place.

Jesus must have thought, "Relating to these people is like trying to relate to a baby!" Does the baby have any sense of how tired, needy, distracted, or trapped, her mother might be? No, the baby sees the mother as the fountain that meets all her needs. An infant is entirely self-seeking and doesn't see a person, just senses a needs-meeting-machine. If the machine runs dry, there is hysteria.

Or maybe he thought, "Relating to these people is like trying to relate to a hormonally-charged adolescent!" Is he seeing his girlfriend as she really is, in all her heartache and complexity, or does he see her through the lens of his own sexual desire and ego needs?

Salome had her own needs and desires all wrapped up in her faith and she missed the point Jesus demonstrated with his own life. He was showing her day by day as he traveled with her and he showed us all, ultimately, on the cross. Paul summed his attitude this way:

*"[Jesus] died for all, that those who live should no longer live for themselves but for him who died for them and was raised again. So from now on we regard no one from a worldly point of view. Though we once regarded Christ in this way, we do so no longer. Therefore, if anyone is in Christ, he is a new creation; the old has gone, the new*

## BUILDING COMMUNITY AS A LIVING ORGANISM

*has come!" (2 Corinthians 5:15)*

That focus is what creates the new community in Christ.

## The cup of suffering and regeneration nourishes the body of Christ

Salome and her boys had a tough time relating to Jesus as he is. They related to him as *they* are. This kind of inability to connect with God and others often wrecks the whole body life Jesus is trying to get going. The same inability could wreck any given meeting of the church if all someone is thinking is, "Give me what I need when I come to church." The same thing could wreck a cell meeting this week, if all someone is hoping is, "Meet my desire."

Jesus seems to have been a little flabbergasted:

*"'You don't know what you are asking,' Jesus said to them. 'Can you drink the cup I am going to drink?'*

*'We can,' they answered.*

*Jesus said to them, 'You will indeed drink from my cup, but to sit at my right or left is not for me to grant. These places belong to those for whom they have been prepared by my Father'".*

James and John did not think this cup Jesus was talking about was a cup of suffering, but that was Jesus' cup. They apparently thought they had already proven themselves and they were ready for the big time — "Didn't we and our mother leave everything and follow you and do what you said all along? When do we get ours?"

Jesus told them, "You'll get yours." James was martyred and John apparently ended his life in exile on a little island. But even before they died they went through a lot of suffering. At this point they wanted to steer the semi, but they were still in driver's ed.

Among Circle of Hope, we often need to remind ourselves that being an organism is not instinctual. People can get in over their heads when they try it. Many people feel like they are driving a semi as soon as they get the keys for making a relationship with us in Christ. It can feel too big to handle; and running over someone is a distinct possibility! A person walked into a meeting not long ago and felt overwhelmed by the love they were seeing. They felt totally unable to share in it — it all just felt painfully good. It will take some time before they can accept that a Jesus-following love goes to Jerusalem, and might stop for a stranger. A person went to one of the cells where he was listened to and suddenly he found himself sharing all sorts of things he had no intention of sharing, things he didn't even feel *allowed* to share. He hadn't realized how no one generally listened to him. Maybe he will soon get used to the fact that God is not just working at getting something out of him, but is genuinely interested in restoring what's built into him. Freely giving love and openly listening are simple things to understand but painful things to practice. We all think they should be normal, but they aren't. We're trying to learn.

That day Jesus was beginning to teach that the only way to be the spiritual organism he is forming is to run on the fuel contained in the cup of *suffering and regeneration* he was talking about. The only way to gain the life he is bringing is to lose the instincts that don't resonate with it. The only way to get inside the kingdom is to stop seeing God like we used to and to see him in Jesus, as he really is — the suffering servant, then the risen Lord. The only way to build community with him is to stop seeing others as we used to, and see them as Jesus sees them — a new creation.

## It takes humility to participate in growing that kind of body

The humility it takes for God to become *like* us and then become a servant *of* us, is the spirit that makes his kind of love possible and what creates the new humanity. The alternative to building that community is obvious and it was obvious that day. It says:

*"When the ten heard about this, they were indignant with the two brothers."*

The grasping for power and the lack of humble love created indignation. The ten were like a chorus of babies: "They're going after my milk!" A choir of teenagers, "He's after my girl!"

I've heard that choir and sung it in many times. No loving community of faith (or marriage, family, or friendship, for that matter) got loving without going through indignation. I lived in an intentional community (an extreme version of who we are as Circle of Hope) for about eight years. Back in the day, in our household, there was plenty of reactivity all the time, even though we were a crew who were quite conversant in community. For instance, one man worked at one of the original Footlockers. He loved shoes. He had a lot of shoes before he moved in. Our community wanted to live simply, so several housemates doubted whether he needed all those shoes and thought he should probably send them to the poor along with all the socks he needed for all his shoes. But he found a lot of comfort in his socks. His mother's family had run around in the Philippines barefoot! Indignation followed. That's what happens when Christ's new organism grows — fights about whether to buy socks! Whenever we go for the fullness of "love one another as I have loved you," there are always many opportunities to learn humility and to serve. If we want to be in the center of Christ culture and not just looking at it from afar; we'll have to risk the suffering included in getting there.

Intentional communities at all levels: families, households, cells, teams, congregations, all test our love and help us practice the suffering and humility it takes to become new and knit together. Our church is intended to help us practice that healing suffering. We know that many people won't be able to enter in automatically and we don't expect them to. We stretch to include people who are just outside the door of faith as well as people who are deep into the house. We have an extensive "porch," you might say, but we also want to keep spawning deeper household arrangements where people can learn and prove the love of God.

Wide or deep, there will still be lots of indignation to endure. I can't count the number of households that never got started, cells that fell apart, and families that disintegrated because people didn't find a Match.com kind of connection with a group that met their desires or vision. It was like they were asking Jesus, just like Salome: "Grant that I will get it MY way." I can't imagine all the people who have left our church because they were betrayed or hurt or disillusioned when we did not meet up to their standards or desires. I wonder if Jesus says to them, "Do you know what you are asking?"

## Jesus had to teach his disciples a lesson and he keeps teaching it

*"You know that the rulers of the Gentiles lord it over them, and their high officials exercise authority over them. Not so with you. Instead, whoever wants to become great among you must be your servant, and whoever wants to be first must be your slave— just as the Son of Man did not come to be served, but to serve, and to give his life as a ransom for many."*

Our perverse instinct is to dominate. We want what we want when we want it, and we have been that way ever since we were babies. Our instinct is to get what we can, like an adolescent boy grabbing for a breast or like a frenzied shopper grabbing what is there before it is gone or before the price goes up. Our instinct is to get some kind of power, like a person who has a lot of power and is preserving it, or like a person who has less power than they want and is always trying to get more. Those instincts are anti-community. Everyone pursuing such things is weakening our organism as we speak.

One of the reasons people often flee from the church is because Christians seem to be so clueless about how they are grasping for power, like James and John were. Why is it that, so often, a congregation is dominated by a strong-willed pastor, or some other leader telling everyone what to do? Somehow he (usually he) gets people to serve him, instead of being a servant. The church ends up being about him, rather than being circled around Jesus.

On the other hand, why is it that, so often, there is a less overt grasping for power going on among the people of the church who are indignant about how they are "dominated" by the powerful? No matter what is done, some people seem to be offended, perpetually waiting to be served as well as they ought to be. Their perpetual criticism, usually communicated indirectly, poisons the atmosphere, and circles people around them, instead of Jesus. It is no surprise that in Paul's lists of sins that kill faith, he usually includes "gossip" and "slander" — the weapons of the supposedly powerless.

Both the strong and the weak have powerful weapons to employ. We have to be careful, lest our ambition for power, masquerading as ambition to be the best we can be, or masquerading as resistance to injustice or inadequacy, ends up undermining the community. We are passionate about having healthy conflicts that lead to a trust system. Jesus leads us to imagine that a new impulse can reign and fuel a new community. Christians have given up on the old instincts and received true life from the hand of Jesus. We are capable of serving.

## Regularity helps us learn to be a new kind of organism in the world

God installs us in an organism that reminds us who we are and stimulates us to do what we can do. I think it should seem strange to say we are convicted that we need to be an organism building community — what else are Christians? But we have to say that to a narcissistic age, condemned to individualism. A lot of people don't know much about community anymore. It is radical to be a normal Christian. How can we do it?

Being a healthy part of the organism starts off with very basic disciplines that keep us in a safe context for further connection to God and others. We always start with the three symbolic meetings that express who we are as a people in Jesus and move on from there. If we can manage these three commitments to build community, we have a good chance of actually overcoming our broken instincts and putting on our new lives as part of the organism that is the body of Christ.

1. We never miss a meeting of our cell, that little intentional community. As we see the others through the eyes of Jesus and are fully ourselves, slowly but surely, we find ourselves acclimating to being part of the organism.

2. We are devoted to the public meeting. It is not just another thing on the schedule. We don't *attend* it; we *are* it. It expresses our

heart, our identity. We learn so much when we worship and listen to God together in public: how to worship with abandon and sense God's presence, while not being focused merely on ourselves, but also on all the others, including the newest person. We end up worshiping as a servant, not as one being served.

3. We always make it to the Love Feast where all the cells and congregations of Circle of Hope celebrate being one in Christ. When we get the whole network together we are a witness to the powers that be that something other than what they control is happening.

The Love Feast is a powerful "in your face" to the domination system. We cross political, racial and social boundaries, we cross territorial, class and other divisions to proclaim that nothing can separate us from the love of Jesus and nothing can keep that love from keeping us together. When we can do that, we're an organism. It's powerful.

As we are keeping these basics covered, we keep our minds and hearts open to even deeper expressions. It usually astounds me that people think our life together is radical. It seems quite basic. Maybe the love of God is more splendid than we usually think! We're grateful for the people who explore the deeper territories of that splendor by intentionally living in community. They might be like our pituitary gland, or some other part of the body I don't understand that seems to make a big difference if it doesn't function well.

Shalom House, the Simple Way, Camden House and other friends in the New Monasticism movement , all the other people who have inventive ways to share in common houses or share life as neighbors, keep reminding us that the Holy Spirit brings us together with God and each other in brilliant ways that reveal God's glory.

Like I keep saying, some of us will be like babies for a long time when it comes to living in the new community Jesus is forming. It is inevitable. You might be in your cell one evening and it seems like you're Elmo and it's time to "ask a baby!" because everyone seems like such a baby (or worse). We love babies. Without a doubt, you will run into a person who seems arrested in adolescence or somewhere else on the development path and you'll be dealing

## BUILDING COMMUNITY AS A LIVING ORGANISM

with that. We love adolescents, age-wise and otherwise. Don't get indignant. You'll run into some St. John of the Cross who met God deeply, was deeply hurt, or both when the church abused their trust. Just drink the cup of suffering and regeneration with Jesus.

Drinking that cup together can have great results. When people are consistently dipped in a community filled with Jesus-love, like some kind of spiritual solvent for hearts hardened by self-destructive instincts, babies are nurtured to wholeness, adolescents make it through the storm, the conflicted have a home to which they can return and the ignorant find patient teachers, just like Zebedee's family did. Just the other night, I was sitting around a table with a new circle of ten, witnessing how the solvent had been working. We were gathered to consider all it means to join in a covenant with the others at the center of our church. Almost everyone seemed to have soaked up the culture of love Jesus has built among us — some had been saturated in a few weeks, others had spent a few years being penetrated. As they articulated what they had sensed and experienced among us, I realized that our info session was like a few flowers on the frosting of the cake. They'd been surrounded by cake for a long time, and they were eating it. That's the result of being an organism feeding on the Spirit and including the wonderful beings Jesus redeems to build it up and strengthen it for the good it can be and do.

CHAPTER 9

# Maintaining the Dialogue
*The Story: Jesus tells the story of the two sons. Luke 15*

Two things are bound to happen if a lot of single Christians build a church together: first, marriages, then babies. We are experiencing both. Droves of babies are entering the scene around here! — crawling herds. But second, at the same time, given how our bodies seem to work these days, there are quite a few couples who are experiencing the pain of infertility, genetic defect and miscarriage. There is a lot of successful cellular communication going on. But there are a surprising number of miscues, too.

As a result of all the pregnancies, I often get to be with prospective fathers for a "father blessing" during which men launch their friend into fatherhood. It includes some deep dialogue you might not expect from the guys. In the same week, I might share the private pain many people suffer in the midst of all the fertility around them. One dear friend has birthed three stillborn children in as many years due to a genetic miscue. He and his wife, along with others, have lead the church to handle grief with honesty and trust. But he can't help thinking that love-sex-pregnancy should come to a better end. Their experience of birth and death has also caused some deep dialogue.

At his father blessing (during the pregnancy of the child who was blessedly born healthy), my friend was excited, nervous and moved by the gravity of being blessed by his loved ones. The "blessing"/ceremony/tribal-council-around-the-fire (it's hard to describe) is quite serious. It stretches the guys. We talk about our own fathers, about how we see the prospective father being a good or not-so-good father; we make promises, we pray. There is lots of talking, and lots of intimacy — both of which make many men feel under-equipped! But the difficulty of speaking heart to heart is why it feels so good afterwards.

The hard work of being ourselves in Christ, taking our place in the circle of love Jesus builds, dealing with life and death and letting ourselves be heard is so weighty! We're participating in creating something with God; it's akin to him speaking the world into being.

A father blessing is a good example of how dialogue creates gravity and how gravity allows dialogue. Dialogue is like a foundry where God shapes us into people who can each express our own kind of "parentness," where "iron sharpens iron" like the proverb promises. Dialogue is how God brings us to "the whole measure of the fullness of Christ," which is why we built a lot of talking into the heart of how we operate as Circle of Hope. When we can sit in the Circle and speak heart to heart, then we will, like Paul says,

*"no longer be infants, tossed back and forth by the waves, and blown here and there by every wind of teaching and by the cunning and craftiness of men in their deceitful scheming. Instead, speaking the truth in love, we will in all things grow up into him who is the Head, that is, Christ. From him the whole body, joined and held together by every supporting ligament, grows and builds itself up in love, as each part does its work." (Ephesians 4:15-16).*

Speaking the truth in love is how we grow up into our fullness in Christ. Speaking the truth in love is how the body is held together, and the absence of it is how it is divided.

Dialogue is our gravity in every sense of the word. The actual words romping back and forth across a room, or the words hitting you like a bullet in the middle of a conflict, may feel like they are knocking you off your feet, at times — but the process of sharing them is what, ultimately, gives us a place to firmly plant our feet in love. When we open up a conversation, the Spirit of God gets a lot of opportunity to plant in the spaces plowed up between us. The dialogue, as out-of-control as it seems, gives God many chances to steer. It seems paradoxical to people who like to keep things quiet and controlled, but encouraging the chaos of open communication increases the number of people who can get into an authentic dialogue in Christ with others. As a result, what might look like chaos to some people is God's chance to grasp all the strands and knit us together in love. That's one of the reasons our website opens with a blog rather than a picture of our building. We hope people will be drawn into our dialogue of love. Our dialogue defines who we are more than our meeting.

In an era of sound bites, in a city where people don't speak to each other on the street, where many people never talk to their neighbors, and where hip restaurants are so loud you can't even hear yourself think, much less have a conversation, having a dialogue of love is a precious ability to learn and a rare skill to practice. But we so desperately need to practice it! A healthy church thrives on a dialogue of love and dies from the lack of it. A dialogue is like a spiritual stretching exercise, at least, and like running a spiritual marathon, at its most challenging. But at every level, they are how a strong body of Christ has authentic life. I find them fascinating, so I guess I am in the right job, since I'm a listener, if I am anything, as a pastor. I listen for Jesus in the revelations from individuals and the revelations happening between them all the time.

In an era when Rupert Murdoch and his competitors vie to create powerful media empires to control the means of communication, a group of men and/or women circled to give a father or a mother blessing is like a subversive act! Cell meetings are revolutionary, since they say, in no uncertain terms, that we are real people who speak the truth in love with Jesus as the owner of our outlet! We have our own sense of what is "news!" No one can blow us around by their cunning or deceit unless we stop having healthy dialogue in Christ.

◂ A CIRCLE OF HOPE

## The Dialogue Between God and Us

One of the most basic and beloved stories Jesus told us to show what relating to God is like is a dialogue between a father and his two sons. When Jesus told the story, God was having a dialogue with humankind in the person of Jesus, who is called "the word" of God.

We say that the Bible contains the Spirit-breathed "word" of God. It is all about dialogue. The church has been talking, for centuries, with God and with one another about what Jesus said the day he told His famous story. And ever since, we have been talking about what Spirit-inspired people have said about what Jesus said! God keeps engaging new people in the conversation. When Jesus first told the story, God was speaking the truth in love by telling a story that teaches us about how God speaks the truth in love with his children.

You probably remember hearing about this broken, hurting family. One son turned away from his father and took his future inheritance into his own hands. He squandered his wealth and ended up homeless and in despair. He decided to return to his father and ask for a job as a hired hand, not hoping to ever be treated as a son again.

"He got up and went to his father. But while he was still a long way off, his father saw him and was filled with compassion for him; he ran to his son, threw his arms around him and kissed him

The son said to him, "Father, I have sinned against heaven and against you. I am no longer worthy to be called your son. Make me like one of your hired men."

But the father said to his servants, "Quick! Bring the best robe and put it on him. Put a ring on his finger and sandals on his feet. Bring the fattened calf and kill it. Let's have a feast and celebrate. For this son of mine was dead and is alive again; he was lost and is found." So they began to celebrate." (Luke 15:20-23)

Jesus lays out a dialogue between a son and his father that paints a picture of the dialogue all of us lost children of God have with God. It is usually something like this:

Child to Father: "I have sinned. I am no longer worthy, though I was made worthy. Please take me back."

Father to Child: "I'll clothe you in my best. I'll give you back your ring of authority and restore your sense of value. Let's have a party. Now you are alive. Now you are found."

For some of us who have never had such a conversation, this dialogue might seem very unrealistic. It might seem more like a very moving scene in a movie, the kind that evokes our deep wishes for the love we never had — like Cecily Tyson running down the road to meet Paul Winfield in *Sounder* (1972) — they still show that on rainy days in elementary school, right?, or seeing Rosario's reaction when she sees Carlitos on the other side of the street in *La Misma Luna* (2007). Playing the part of the son in the Lord's story might be very difficult for some people — even though honestly blurting things out things like he did can feel pleasantly cathartic. Playing the part of the Father might *really* be tough! But that is the part we are called to play when we are told to speak the truth in love. We are called to be humble, gracious, open and joyful — and speak it! To get to the Parent part, play the child part, first.

We are created to be as awesome, in the best sense of that word, as the Father is in the story. Dialogue among Christians is very grave like that, with all the life and death overtones that "grave" should have. In our conversations we are taking each other very seriously! We are bringing each other to life. To work with God in growing each other up into Christ, dialogue must be practiced very deliberately — and it must be done in an environment where risk is required and discernment expected. Our words are not things we can take lightly. They are dangerous — like what I remember of sulfuric acid. I once worked in a lab where I had to clean the lab ware with sulfuric acid. I had to be sure not to forget and combine the acid with water because that would have had explosive results! Just a drop of acid splattered in a wet sink popped like a firecracker! (which, of course, I tried, so I could see what would happen). Caring for new creations takes as much concentration as handling nuclear rods in the reactor. They are awesome. It is a grave work.

So one would think that the church, in general, would be full of skilled practitioners! You'd think our splendid dialogue of love would be one of the main ways people see Jesus in us. Much the contrary, one of the main reasons there are so many "former Christians" and nominal believers who can't relate to the church is that people could not speak the truth in love. What's more, in the U.S., where everyone speaks the language called "advertising," people have been turned off by the lack of truth in the church's advertising. We talk about love all the time and then the congregation blows apart in conflict! So many churches have been undermined by liars and taken over by judgers that people can't stand the thought of being a part of one. I think one of the main reasons Christianity became something people think is a "private" matter is because they despaired of ever managing to talk about it in public without getting slammed, flamed, preached at, or ridiculed — and that's just by the church people! Some denominations actually built mistrust into their polity by instituting the same structure of checks and balances built into the U.S. government to accommodate our basic assumption that people are can't be trusted.

## So what do we do when it doesn't work so well?

Jesus acknowledges the reality that people live in a state of broken dialogue and that they despair of having it repaired. Right after he lays out a tender reunion scene between a father and son, he brings in the other side with another son. As soon as speaking the truth in love is restored in the family, the practice is threatened. There is a lot of plowing to do before love takes root in a family like ours, too.

Here's the rest of the story.

Out in the field, an older son is working (unlike what his younger brother ever did!). He hears the sound of music. He comes in to the house and immediately feels left out of the loop because a party is going on. He has to ask one of the servants what is happening in his own home! The servant tells him. "Your brother has been found. Your father has killed the best calf and we're having a feast."

## MAINTAINING THE DIALOGUE

The older brother is so mad he won't even go inside! Here's what happened:

*His father went out and pleaded with him.*

This father must be getting tired! He ran down the road to meet one son, organized a party, and now he dashes out of the celebration to plead with his other son! He reminds me of the mediator I met in South Africa who had done a great job teaching violence-replacing dialogue to people in some of Capetown's toughest neighborhoods. He said, "The best mediator is a bridge who gets walked on from both directions." This poor father and our Father could surely relate to getting himself walked on! His other son was used to having his disgraceful brother out of the picture and now Dad's sitting down with him chatting over cheesesteaks! Getting the two sons together was going to be tough.

*"[The son] answered his father, 'Look! All these years I've been slaving for you and never disobeyed your orders. Yet you never gave me even a young goat so I could celebrate with my friends. But when this son of yours who has squandered your property with prostitutes comes home, you kill the fattened calf for him!'*

*"My son," the father said, "you are always with me, and everything I have is yours. But we had to celebrate and be glad, because this brother of yours was dead and is alive again; he was lost and is found.'" (Luke 15:28-31)*

Jesus lays out another dialogue between a son and his father that gives a picture of the dialogue all us lost children of God have with God:

Child to Father: "I'm angry. I'm hurt. I feel betrayed. I do the right things but things don't work out right. I have legitimate expectations and you don't do what I expect. You don't punish predictably or give consistently."

Father to Child: "You are always with me. All I have is yours. Come celebrate with me. Come be with your brother. He was lost and now he's found. He was dead, now he's alive. That's what's important. It is not just between you and me. It is not just about you. It's about all of us."

We all come to the party late, whether we're out talking to swine or out making business calls. We're all late and we are all so hurt! Our families hurt us. Our previous lovers hurt us. Our present loved ones keep doing it. Our defenses against all this pain are so good, even God has to chase us down to get a hearing. *Jesus* even seems threatening!

It is no wonder that speaking the truth in love, like a member of God's family might do, is difficult. One needs to feel secure to do it. One needs to feel important to the "tribe" to speak up as if she might be taken seriously. We don't even have enough courage to insert ourselves into a little circle of people talking at a party or after the church meeting unless one of the people in the circle looks at us over someone's shoulder and gives us some kind of affirming signal that it is OK to enter! We're so tender from our many bruises that we need a lot of tenderness.

One of the commenters on this chapter said: "The point about feeling secure enough to speak truth in love is key. If I don't feel like people are listening to me, I stubbornly clam right up. I am an introvert at heart, and I am not keen to make people listen to me. When I first got here to Circle I needed to be invited in to fully participate in everything from a cell to leading our church. And, thank God, I was invited! That makes me even more aware of those who may not feel connected, and I try to reach out and link them in so they, too, can offer their truth to us."

No person can give us enough tenderness to makes us brave enough to enter into the fullness of love. We need the embrace of God. But we can certainly be on God's side! We are called to be embracers, just like our Father! Among the circles of Circle of Hope, we keep trying to nurture an environment where everyone gets a chance keep replaying the dialogue between God and his children until we can feel how it works again. One of the ways we try to stay in that territory is to give each other an opportunity to bind ourselves together in a covenant of love so each of us can have some level of confidence that we will be taken seriously. We even have a ceremony (full of talking, of course) in which people are publicly welcomed into our expanding circle. We want to have an agreement "up front" that we can rely on each other to listen and stick with us, even when we don't know what we are talking about. All of us can think of a lot of reasons why we shouldn't be accepted. It helps if our environment keeps convincing us that it is OK to open our mouths.

## Take the Risk to Talk

Love takes risk. We are called to keep putting our love out there in the ongoing dialogue and trust it to be tossed into the salad God keeps serving for dinner. Even when we "thought we'd heard it all," even when we "can't believe our ears," even when we face "oh snap," we are called to believe that speaking the truth in love is what keeps us rooted in God and growing into our fullness. Just like we stay in our dialogue with God — we "pray without ceasing," we stay in our dialogue with each other — "speaking the truth in love."

Some people can slice you like a scalpel with a few sentences. Some can soothe you completely with a cluck. Some seem to be wielding a blunt instrument in their mouth. Some fill you with joy at the sound of their happiness. To put that all together and make pleasant music that reflects the Lord's grace takes a lot of determination. You have to run after it when its coming up the road or stuck in the back yard..

We'll all probably have interesting variations on the theme of what makes that music hard to produce. For instance:
- You may have the shame gene. I'm still working with it. I can hardly help but tell a lie about myself, I am so afraid that someone will be displeased with me! I am still looking for the affirmation of my parents I somehow missed.
- Some of us have tongue paralysis. A person recently left our community after more than five years among us without one honest word to his cell, who had struggled and loved him for a year. He couldn't bring himself to communicate.
- We get blinded by injustice. People have gotten divorced

# A CIRCLE OF HOPE

among us. Part of the reason they separated is that they had no commitment to honest communication and had no humility in the face of not being able to do it. Partners were resolutely on either side of a power struggle and thought their sense of justice made sense.

- We think protecting our identity is crucial. People "find themselves" in a lot of ways, and it isn't always through a dialogue with God. As a result, many people separate from the church because they feel different, or just plain righter than the rest of us. They might as well be Warren G and Adina endlessly looping, "What's love got to with it?" They're more subject to the "it" of their thinking than the "us" of God's people.

We explored the art of dialogue in a public meeting one time. Predictably, we forced people to break into little groups to talk it over. One man immediately walked out! He is such an introvert he was blown away by being coerced into relating. He was hardly the first to run, but he might have been the most honest, since he at least came back later and told me why he fled! It is tempting to never put anyone through such things, even though the Bible seems to imply that God is very interested in us doing them!

We try not to give in to the pressure to stop talking, even though that poor man gets uncomfortable, even though some people think *anonymous* is safe and we want them to feel safe, even though some people think *alone* is existential reality and we hate to confront them. We are going to keep forcing the issue. We don't want to keep truth and love locked up in some predictable, controllable format that one can visit like visiting a lion at the zoo. God can't be caged. Dialogue in Christ can't be reduced to a performance piece or a book of principles rather than relating to a person! We are going to stick our heads in the lion's mouth and trust God for whatever happens.

Lord, knows. We might get our heads bit off! We want to risk offending those who never say anything lest someone be offended. We want to face those who are always so offended that it feels risky to talk to them. Dialogue is like mouth-to-mouth resuscitation for people dying for lack of love and truth in their lives. We have to rush in with the breath of life — something like our Father and His children.

One of our commenters talked about learning to rush in.
"I believe that I am secure in Christ and I have made the pact as a Cell Leader to dialogue and yet speaking the truth in love is still the hardest thing for me to do. I think the root of my inaction is really insecurity. I know that I am safe and yet I don't feel it. Fear preempts the dialogue that is needed to grow each other up.

I have a couple of friends who suffer from panic/anxiety disorders. The cure, I'm told, is a gradual acceptance of the anxious feelings that are exaggerated by the disorder. These folks know they are safe. They can tell themselves they are loved, but when moments of intense anxiety occur, it is very hard to remember that they are safe— that they are loved. The best way to recover is to expose oneself intentionally to anxiety-inducing situations and go through the fear. The hope is that you will adjust to the way your emotions and your body react to stimuli in order to correct the imbalance that has bubbled up for whatever reason (psychologists correct me, please).

To a lesser degree I suffer from that anxiety [when it comes to dialogue]…"

## Do what it takes to communicate, or die

Dialogue is so basic to being a follower of Jesus that we "bet the farm," so to speak, as Circle of Hope, on learning how to do it. We tried to build fail-safe devices into our structure, even, that would *make* us do it — either we learn to speak the truth in love, or we disintegrate. And we ought to disintegrate, if we don't communicate! We certainly don't want to amaze the world again by being another "miraculous" church that can hold together without love or even relationship!

Our Cell Leaders all agree to communicate at all costs. They even wrote it down in their "pact." The Cell Leaders commit to "maintain open dialogue, learning and practicing the skills of directly speaking the truth in love; we have healthy conflicts with members of the leadership team directly; we openly promote and demonstrate our deliberate attempts to live in a 'trust system" (*Cell Plan*, see page 32). We try to remember that *how* we say something is at least as important as *what* we say. We hold one another more accountable for a life of love than we are offended by a slip of the tongue.

This sounds great on paper! It sounded great when Jesus taught it and when his disciples made some important summary of what he taught in Matthew 18, too. That doesn't mean it works great in practice. All the Cell Leaders could probably tell the story of a time when they were so frustrated with someone that they totally forgot their pact and talked about the frustrating person with someone else before they had even talked to them! They could also tell you how many times they succumbed to the temptation to slip on the guise of therapist (we love therapists) and pretend they were one, so their friends could have the freedom of their "confidentiality" to gossip or slander, rather than being appalled that someone would drag them into such a compromise of love in the name of "trust."

I wish we would get as "up in arms" about the lack of speaking the truth in love like we get "up in arms" about governments that are literally up to their eyeballs in the use of arms! Because the tongue is a powerful little weapon, too. The tongue is a fire and people have already had their hand on the stove. I always suggest the same few practices for helping people recover from being burned so often.

- Never speak for someone who is not there. For instance, "*Several people* told me you were very mean to Brittney!" Let the *several people* have their own voice. If someone tells you what someone else said, go find out from them if they said it before you believe it.
- Try to be direct. Let your "yes be yes." An example of indirectness might be, "I told you I felt bad and you did nothing!" Instead of trying to imagine what people leave unsaid, let people ask for what they want. Dropping hints and not being responsible for our own desires and demands is understandable (we've been hurt!) but it is still kind of infantile. It is nice of us to be parental,

but our goal is to help each other grow up in Christ, not keep each other locked in immature patterns.
- Don't rehearse conflict with someone other than the one who offends you. For instance, "Phil dominated the conversation all night and I couldn't get a word in edgewise!" Phil might be saying about you, "Amanda sat over in the corner all night while I was spilling my guts and wouldn't even give me one word of comfort!" It is bad enough that people have a hard time hearing each other. Not talking to them, but talking to everyone else about them, causes *more* people to misunderstand and erodes everyone's dignity. Try letting people be innocent, or prospectively repentant, until they personally prove they are guilty.
- Don't be so naïve as to think that your group of sympathizers won't easily become a divisive faction. An example of how these things get started might be saying to your group of cronies (who might all be dressed like you, or something), "Circle is all hipsters!" or maybe, "The parents are taking over the church!" or even, "What's with all this dialogue!" Who wants to be unwittingly responsible for forming the hipster faction or the parents' clique or the dialogue detractors?!

## Speak the Truth in Love

Some places have "truth" — it screams down on you like an interrogation light, as if you were a criminal; it assesses you rationally, like one might a microbe; it judges you, as if you are probably an infidel, guilty until proven innocent. It kills.

Some places have "love" — it says nothing, as if you can't be trusted to understand; it knows "whatever" as if you wouldn't be able to relate to something that was not exactly like yourself; it affirms everything as if you would be offended at almost anything. It ends up a vacuous, fear-inducing lie.

Truth and love need to go together as we speak to each other, like the Bible says and like God demonstrates in Jesus. Then gravity forms. All of us are responsible for our part in forming it.

### A CIRCLE OF HOPE

Maybe we underestimate just how unusual forming gravity is. I was talking to our landlord the other day, with whom we started a relationship like WWE wrestlers might, literally screaming at each other, at times, about the problems with our interrelated building projects. We have since become better friends. But our relationship isn't held together by Christ. Our bonding centers more on memories of all the times our contractors have ripped us off or walked off unfinished jobs. Recently, I complained to him that I needed to find a lawyer to deal with a collection agency that would not leave us alone about a bill we did not incur. He said we didn't need a lawyer, we could just put him on the phone and he could threaten them with a visit from a couple of his close friends (that's South Philly Italian talk). That's typical. Our conversation was littered with the lies and hate we have experienced, and with the subterfuge, violence, deception and bullying out of which we often respond!

Speaking the truth in love is among those world-changing aspects of Christianity that rarely get tried, it seems so extreme. But people often take notice when someone surprises them by doing it. My most-viewed MySpace blog entry (in one day, at least) was a re-post of a Joan Chittister article from the *Catholic Review*. She was reflecting on the Nickel Mines shooting of Amish girls (October, 2006).

*It was not the violence suffered by the Amish community last week that surprised people. Our newspapers are full of brutal and barbarian violence day after day after day — both national and personal. What really stunned the country about the attack on the small Amish schoolhouse in Pennsylvania was that the Amish community itself simply refused to hate what had hurt them. …It was not the murders, not the violence, that shocked us; it was the forgiveness that followed it for which we were not prepared. It was the lack of recrimination, the dearth of vindictiveness that left us amazed. Baffled. Confounded. It was the Christianity we all profess but which they practiced that left us stunned. Never had we seen such a thing.*

Many of the Amish took their unwanted moment in the spotlight to speak the truth in love, even as parents of lost children. They thought they should try it. Astounding! Had we, as a country, followed their example as a nation after 9/11, the impact might have been earth-shattering. If we all act like those dear people after we leave our public meeting this week, especially when we meet people out on the sidewalk in front of our buildings, and particularly when we live with our families and work with our mates, we might have an equally seismic impact. We all need to come to the party and add our voice. We need to believe that what we add to the dialogue makes a difference.

Our ability to say what we mean and mean what we say in a way that smells of love is the gravity that keeps our feet on the way of life. It is our drawing power, and the lack of it is what spins people out of their orbit around the Lord. The story that is told about what each of us says and how all of us manage to work out our lives in love should be full of bafflingly beautiful examples of speaking the truth in love like our Father.

CHAPTER 10

# Fomenting Diversity and Reconciliation
*The Story: Jesus and the women — in Lebanon and Samaria, Mark 7 and John 4*

I can't tell if I am as big a failure as I feel I am or surprisingly successful. I am surrounded by many amateur, and some professional, sociologists who regularly bomb our church with statistics: "You are in a half-black city; why aren't you half black? Your neighborhood is filling with Spanish, Cambodian, et al speakers; why aren't you saying the Lord's prayer in Khmer? You seem to still be a white male...in 2007!" (Actually, my great-grandparents were registered Choctaws, so I prefer "so-called white male"). I do not kid you, many people walk into our meetings on Sunday night and are immediately deflated when their head count of people of color does not meet up to their desires. I am a failure at diversity.

It doesn't do any good to enumerate how many black, Asian, Hispanic, Russian or Presbyterian friends and comrades I have (which seems like such a weird thing to do, I'd hate to start), nor to remind the critic that "as the church" we actually do have ways we're relating across obvious boundaries: we're connected to non-English speakers in all sorts of ways — including ESOL classes, we have a reconciliation team that works to undermine systemic racism, and we keep supporting a church planting efforts among the next generation in all sorts of neighborhoods. That doesn't mention that homeless people, unbelieving people, gay people, transsexual people, democrats, republicans, high-powered professionals, punks, bonafide hipsters and conservative grandmothers were all at our last Love Feast. I am actually surprisingly successful. We are working at being diverse, if anyone is. But the judgment remains.

On the darkside of postmodernism there still lurks a language in which people are beans and truth is bean counting. Nowhere is this more pronounced than when talking about race. But we keep talking. If we are fools for Christ, this must be the core expression of our identity. We keep throwing ourselves into the fire of the great national sin. And we regularly feel a bit more than singed. After ten-plus years of failing to produce the TV-ad picture of multicultural harmony in one of the most divided-up cities in the country, we still can't get it out of our minds that God would love to breech the divisions in any number of ways, and we might even get to the place where a big happy family can live in actual community by sharing a common Spirit.

## The New Humanity

We want to be the new humanity. So we say we are perpetually conducting a dialogue on diversity. The apostle Paul got us going. When he talked about the chasm between Jews and Gentiles, he wrote to the Ephesians:

*In Christ Jesus you who once were far away have been brought near through the blood of Christ. "For he himself is our peace, who has made the two one and has destroyed the barrier, the dividing wall of hostility, by abolishing in his flesh the law with its commandments and regulations. His purpose was to create in himself one new **man** [we say "humanity" or "person"] out of the two, thus making peace, and in this one body to reconcile both of them to God through the cross, by which he put to death their hostility. He came and preached peace to you who were far away and peace to those who were near. For through him we both have access to the Father by one Spirit. (Ephesians 2:13-18)*

In his letter to the Colossians he extended the idea beyond just Jews and Gentiles to cover all the divisions he could imagine:

*Do not lie to each other, since you have taken off your old self with its practices and have put on the new self, which is being renewed in knowledge in the image of its Creator. Here* [and we think of ourselves as a "here"] *there is no Greek or Jew, circumcised or uncircumcised, barbarian, Scythian, slave or free, but Christ is all, and is in all. (Colossians 3:9-11)*

## The Possible Dream

In 2006, PW Botha died. He was well-known in South Africa and around the world for holding the line against dismantling apartheid, despite economic sanctions that crippled his country. His death gave the post-apartheid government an opportunity to display the magnanimity that prevented South Africa from collapsing into violence in the 1990s. Former President Nelson Mandela was reported as saying, "While to many Mr. Botha will remain a symbol of apartheid, we also remember him for the steps he took to pave the way towards the eventual peacefully negotiated settlement in our country." President Thabo Mbeki announced that flags would be flown at half mast until the eve of the funeral, to mark the death of a former head of state. The offer of a state funeral was declined by Botha's family. A private funeral was held in the town of George where Botha was buried. Mbeki attended the funeral. Acts like that make dreams of the new humanity possible. Bishop Desmond Tutu and thousands of other Christians worked very hard in South Africa, like Mandela and Mbeki, to give the new humanity a chance.

It is a hard lesson to learn. I am encouraged that the Lord Jesus seemed to learn the lesson himself, one day. Magnanimity and inclusion are traits that holy people acquire on the journey through this divided up world. They start in their own territory, but gradually the wide-open spaces of the Kingdom of God become more and more apparent and preferred. I first heard this interpretation of Mark 7 in Colombia, right before I mistakenly ate lettuce washed in local water. So my own "dream of liberation" may be colored by stomach cramps, but the slant has seemed more and more apt, ever since.

In Mark 7 we learn that Jesus left his usual itineration among the people of Israel and went way up north *"to the vicinity of Tyre. He entered a house and did not want anyone to know it; yet he could not keep his presence secret. In fact, as soon as she heard about him, a woman whose little daughter was possessed by an evil spirit came and fell at his feet. The woman was a Greek, born in Syrian Phoenicia. She begged Jesus to drive the demon out of her daughter."*

Jesus is a stranger in a strange land, keeping himself a secret among the Jewish Diaspora, until one of the local Greek-speakers, and a woman, to boot, outs him. He responds to her request with a very predictable reply for a Jewish rabbi. *"First let the children eat all they want,"* he told her, *"for it is not right to take the children's bread and toss it to their dogs."*

Let's say that reply is not as insulting as it sounds. The woman seems to take it as merely a colorful way to make a point about their obvious spiritual and ethnic diversity. Maybe she even takes it as a test to see whether she knows something about who Jesus really is. She seems to have a good idea, because she calls out his deepest nature, *"Yes, Lord,"* she replied, *"but even the dogs under the table eat the children's crumbs."*

It is hard to say just what is happening in-between a few lines of dialogue in Mark's report. But doesn't it seem to you like Jesus is learning something in this moment? I know a lot of us have a perfectionist streak in us that likes Jesus immutable; we like him to be one of those wizened babies in a Renaissance painting lifting up two pudgy little fingers to bless us. But I think he is God being a human, and learning is part of that. In this instance Jesus learns that his mission is truly world-wide. He is learning just how much Israel, in his own person, is meant to be a light to the Gentiles. His mission may begin in his own ethnic/religious culture but it stretches to encompass people considered as good as dogs by his culture.

So he told her, *"For such a reply, you may go; the demon has left your daughter."* And perhaps the demon left Jesus alone after that, too, fully defeated. Not that Jesus was possessed, but he was tempted, like all of us, yet without sin, by the spirit of racism, ethnic hatred, division, indifference. He overcame it. It is possible.

## But it is surely not easy to live reconciled

We have been trying to get some reconciliation going, and we are only modestly successful. That shouldn't be too surprising. We, as individuals and we as members of people groups with histories and reputations, have deeply hurt others and we are deeply hurt. It makes us mad when people don't respond to our attempts to love. It makes us mad when people don't love us. We revert to power. We lust for power. We can't see any way out but to exercise power.

Jesus couldn't even get his own disciples to stop channeling this natural reaction, even though they traveled as the diverse community he had called out. After his famous, boundary-breaking conversation recorded in John 4 with the woman at the well in Samaria (which, to be honest, has been used as an example for about every postmodern wish) his disciples thought he needed to be carted off and protected from himself.

In John 4, Jesus shows again how hard it is to get God to do what you think he should be doing. Instead of serenely waiting in prayer, or something, while the disciples go off to town to find lunch, he violates any taboos a rabbi might observe and talks to a woman — and a *wanton* woman at that, and a wanton *Samaritan* woman, on top of that. You can look up all the details about Samaritans, but let it suffice that the Jews of Jesus' day didn't like Samaritans mainly because they were an insult to God and country. They had a variant version of Judaism with their own religious center to rival Jerusalem. To the mainstream Jews, that made them wicked, unclean and likely-to-defile-you. So it is a big deal that Jesus is taking a drink of water from the hand of this woman. He apparently has a different vision of how the world works.

"*Just then his disciples returned and were surprised to find him talking with a woman. But no one asked, 'What do you want?' or*

'Why are you talking with her?'"

They were too dumbfounded to talk to their leader, but they apparently had a conversation with each other about what was going on! Maybe it was like the hushed conversation whites have about *wannabe black* whites and blacks have about what some people used to call oreos when people aren't around.

Meanwhile, the woman is crossing boundaries right back at Jesus by getting the village to come out and see the Jewish rabbi.

"*Leaving her water jar, the woman went back to the town and said to the people, 'Come, see a man who told me everything I ever did. Could this be the Christ?' They came out of the town and made their way toward him.*"

The disciples remain confused or just indifferent to the whole situation. Or maybe it is, "I'm not going *there!*" They talk to Jesus about *lunch!* When they offer him something to eat, he finally gets frustrated with them and says, "*I have food to eat that you know nothing about.*"

I don't mean to make the guys look too bad, but when they hear what Jesus says, it honestly appears that they wonder what food someone else gave Jesus while they were not looking! "Where is the knapsack in which he is hiding the M and Ms and why won't he give me any?"

"'*My food,' said Jesus, 'is to do the will of him who sent me and to finish his work. Do you not say, "Four months more and then the harvest"? I tell you, open your eyes and look at the fields! They are ripe for harvest.*'"

The harvest is coming up the path from Sychar as they speak. The disciples can not even see it. It is like they are still on the interstate buzzing right over a poor neighborhood, and still not wondering why interstates always seem to cut up poor neighborhoods. It is like they are walking down the street and they hear someone speaking another language, so they blank her out. It is like someone is a different color so they assume they are irrelevant. They had been set up by everything they knew, even the habits of their families' hearts, to be justifiably unreconciled.

But apparently, Jesus' work crosses right over those boundaries. Many Samaritans became believers after Jesus spent two days with them. They told the woman, *"We no longer believe just because of what you said; now we have heard for ourselves, and we know that this man really is the Savior of the world."*

## We want to say we did a few things to live reconciled

We always quote John Perkins saying that *"A gospel that does not reconcile is no gospel at all."* That's a great slogan that takes a miracle to embody. We are into a deeply spiritual work, not just sociological realignments. Whether we succeed or fail, we hope we'll be able to confidently say we did a few things to reflect God's determination to create the new humanity:

<u>We persevered</u>. If we can stick with a long process, maybe something will change. We need endurance and patience to intentionally build relationships based on Christ and to overcome the wounds of prejudice, paternalism, mistrust and systemic racism. It is less a matter of changing our minds and more a matter of managing to stick with some relationships in the same locale for more than a few years.

We often recite the litany of our failures at bridging the white/black divide in Philly. In 1998, I got a grant that allowed us to hire an associate of color. Gerry and I did this great rap together one night that used Psalm 103 as the basis! But when I was in South Africa with a group of African Americans, they advised me that the way our relationship was going had less to do with race and more to do with work ethic. We parted ways. Then we went a different direction, got more money from the denomination and a foundation and did a country-wide search for a person of color who would plant a church, spawned from the one we had already planted. Joe was from a cell church in Virginia. When I met him in the train station at Washington DC, I thought he might just be crazy enough to make it work. He did get something started in Germantown. He did understand us. But he got burned out quick with the challenge of it all and moved to Seattle (it was a popular destination for our friends for a while — we almost had Circle of Hope Seattle!). The little church he left was maneuvered into a merger with another cell church, led by Mike, an African American from Philly who was bivocational. We did OK for a while, even though we discovered that most of the people who came with Mike were also in other more traditional congregations. Mike got ill and we left the further development to Bryan. Bryan was always the most logical leader and had been a part of our efforts from the beginning. He's still trying to work something out. But the congregation imploded with some problems that really make me wonder. As I write, Bryan is trying to find a core group of young people to form the next generation of the church in Germantown. He's persevering. All of us are.

<u>We were flexible</u>. If we can keep changing, maybe true transformation will emerge. Obviously, building the NEW humanity requires responses that may feel uncomfortable, since they are new and truly next. Any living organism, even the body of Christ, tends to revert to familiar patterns. We're not just following our instincts, even newly formed ones; we are trying to follow Jesus.

We don't generally know we are not flexible; we might even think what we reflexively do is, by nature, flexible. More, likely, to be flexible means change will have to get stuffed into the routine by the leaders. That's why our PM leaders are charged to keep what we do as multicultural as they can, even when it means they look like cross-cultural posers. That's not easy. The society keeps saying unified pluralism is good. But the market keeps dividing us into smaller and smaller "niches." Just look at MySpace profiles and see how people define their band's style of music. There is a lot more than race that makes us mutually exclusive, these days!

<u>We ruthlessly but gently evaluated</u>. If we can keep asking the hard questions, maybe we'll eventually accept the answers. We don't evaluate to perfect our sense of judgment; we've got plenty of that already. We keep checking to see if we are still conscious.

One of the interesting things Barak Obama is working at is how to be a person who doesn't fit into traditional categories of race, while navigating the history of race relations in the U.S. Our country is slowly changing its mind about race, but in Philly we have entrenched divisions that don't shift easily. We would like to think that the church of Jesus Christ is a place where race is irrelevant in relation to love and dignity. But in our neighborhood, everyone automatically scopes out where they are acceptable and where they aren't before there is any sharing or love and dignity. Asians stick with Asians, Mexicans with Mexicans, and Philly-bred Africans Americans are especially protective of their territory. There are good reasons for all these things that are hard to overcome. We have to stay aware of them, or they run us.

One person read this chapter and replied like this: "Just this morning in the Magazine section of the Philadelphia Inquirer the front page article is reviewing two documentaries that will be shown tonight dealing with injustice. 'Tonight at 10:00 on WHYY TV12, *Banished* journeys southward to visit communities that expelled all their black citizens at gunpoint in different incidents about 100 years ago.' It feels like more and more the truth is coming out. For there to be reconciliation the truth must be spoken. I do long for reconciliation. I do believe that we become more whole and healed as we work towards the kingdom on earth, the church, being a place of every tribe and language and people and nation (Revelation 5:9). I long for this because I know it is true, and I long for this as the mother of two beautiful trans-racially adopted boys."

<u>We were sincere</u>. If we can stay vulnerable and honest, trust may grow. This means suffering and sacrifice may grow, as well. This means irony and other forms of denial and self-protection will be threatened. You can see why Paul essentially calls the love that reconciles the basic trait of a new creature in Christ:

*"We regard no one from a worldly point of view. Though we once regarded Christ in this way, we do so no longer. Therefore, if anyone is in Christ, he is a new creation; the old has gone, the new has come! All this is from God, who reconciled us to himself through Christ and gave us the ministry of reconciliation." (2 Cor. 5:16-18)*

<u>We were sensitive</u>. We do not merely practice the so-called

political "tolerance" that turns everyone into nothing in order to pretend equality is happening. If we can listen to each other and seek mutual understanding in the context of ongoing interdependence, we can minimize the threat presented by change and by having big ideas.

<u>We were faithful</u>. If a "critical mass" believes we must live reconciled, it will happen. Many people must be able to answer: "Why are we building a diverse cell?" and "Why are our worship times so eclectic in style?" or any of many questions that need to be answered. One typical response will be: "We intentionally go against the divided ways of our society because a diverse church fully represents the kingdom of God! We are part of the transcultural, transnational body of Christ! We are a circle of hope in Jesus Christ open to all people, a safe place to experience, share and express God's love."

## There are many things each of us can do to make a difference.

A lot of people have good ideas. Things change when people act. We care about right thinking, but we care more that people do something with the passion they have. We think there are some essential actions we can take to build the new humanity:

<u>Tell the Jesus story</u>. For real change to happen, people have to trust Jesus. Manny Ortiz says, "The church's task is neither to destroy nor to maintain ethnic identities but to replace them with a new identity in Christ that is more foundational than earthly identities." We are all Jesus in Samaria. We are all Syro-Phoenicians getting to know Jesus.

<u>Make relationships across boundaries</u>. That means overcoming accumulated barriers, making persistent efforts, getting beyond the inevitable conflicts.

<u>Create interdependence</u>. We not only need one another because we are called by God to be one in Christ, we need one another's gifts and struggles to be fully ourselves in Christ.

<u>Sacrifice</u>. Selflessness breeds love. On a personal level, caring

## FOMENTING DIVERSITY AND RECONCILIATION

for another before oneself takes time and effort. What's more, on a public level, demanding that the domination system become just is never popular; it may require getting into trouble. People who dominate in one context or another will have to deliberately share their privileges.

<u>Outdo one another in showing honor</u>. Showing honor empowers another person (or group or race) to lay aside anger and blame in order to create a relationship of trust. Justice grows best in a field of mutual repentance and forgiveness.

<u>Pray</u>. The whole idea takes a miracle.

Some days we seem so diverse, my head swims, "We are way too successful at this. Don't give me more, Lord!" I'm about to have a party with people from Puebla, Mexico. We're getting to know an Indonesian church down Broad St. A group of young, professional African Americans held a big party in our space not long ago. A Liberian just stopped by. A man wants to start a Spanish-speaking Circle of Hope. I love the excitement of the kingdom of God.

But then two drunk, homeless men wander in to get warm while our young, blonde worship leader is timidly leading her song. A black partner in ministry asks me to go with him to make a house deal, since he suspects the realtor is not dealing with him because he is black. An idealistic college grad comes into the meeting expecting to find what he's shopping for in the way of multicultural experiences and we don't measure up. I find out that some Irish enclaves in Philly still have a chip on their shoulder. Another Korean grocer is murdered in his store. Someone assumes I'm just another white person. It is tempting to aspire to easier things.

CHAPTER **11**

# Expressing Our New Selves
*The Story: Jesus and Nicodemus, John 3*

One day, when I was going to make a speech about revealing the best God has built into us, our landlord locked us out of our building. So I stood on a milk crate on the sidewalk outside our door and shouted into the evening air while cars roared by and the subway periodically rumbled underneath. I was a little self-conscious about standing on a milk crate. It was hard to hear what I was trying to say. I thought those gathered were looking at me quizzically — like they expected me to fall off my perch any second and that would be even *more* embarrassing. Some of the people passing by on the sidewalk were a little curious — I didn't look like the usual guy who gets up on a milk crate now and then on the sidewalks of Philly. The people passing in their cars didn't even slow down.

On the one hand, it was a cool, memorable moment. We were kicked to the street, "persecuted" by our landlord, giving it all we've got, expressing ourselves. We were "out there" being Christians. It felt kind of scary and right and appropriately embarrassing. On the other hand, it was not a very effective moment. Our expression seemed to have no impact at all. We couldn't hear each other. We felt worship-naked without our electronica. The passersby not only didn't bother about us much, a good number of them were speaking Spanish and wouldn't have known what we were saying even if they could have heard it!

I suppose, if I had my way, the immigrants from Puebla passing by (some of whom we later met, BTW) would have been stopped in their tracks by a meaningful rendition of the great memory verse from John 3:16: *"Porque tanto amó Dios al mundo, que dio a su Hijo unigénito, para que todo el que cree en él no se pierda, sino que tenga vida eterna."* Now if I could just learn more Spanish!

That famous verse has always been considered good place to start when one wants to reveal Jesus. But I think we might do better to ponder the much-neglected sentences *after* John 3:16 if we want to express anything relevant about Jesus and us these days. What Jesus teaches me in the next verses has helped me wonder how to accept and express the life that is burning in me and pulsing through our body, as Circle of Hope. If you went to Sunday school you probably memorized John 3:16 (or you've at least held it up at a football game — we know you're out there!) But it may be time to memorize some more.

In case you didn't get to the post-John 3:16 verses in Sunday School (the 5% of you who had that experience and were conscious during it), try installing the verses below. If nothing else, memorizing gets us in touch with the ancestors, who were not trained to be applications of a theory or devotees of a principle. The Bible used to be transmitted mouth to ear before people could read, you know. When Jesus told his first followers an important truth, they took pains to remember it — no PDA (that's no *personal digital assistant*, not the *other* PDA, of which there was plenty). Maybe there were papyrus daytimers kept by highly effective people back then, too, but it does not appear to be so. People were not reading and abstracting so much, yet. They were listening and remembering. I've got a feeling they knew less but knew more than most of us.

So take a minute and imagine getting this word from Jesus the old-school way. Listen to what Jesus is expressing about how spiritual life gets expressed. Read these lines out loud, as if they were being said to you. Listen to the sound reverberating in deep receptors.

*"Flesh gives birth to flesh, but spirit gives birth to spirit.*

*You should not be surprised at my saying, `You must be born again.'*

*The wind blows wherever it pleases.*

*You hear its sound, but you cannot tell where it comes from or where it is going.*

*So it is with everyone born of the Spirit."*

This was the great word Jesus gave to Nicodemus the night the Jewish religious leader sneaked out of the house and went to meet the Lord. For us, it is a well from which we draw one of our deep convictions as Circle of Hope. We say: *We expect people to express their gifts, talents, art and worship.*

We expect people to become expressers of the Spirit of God. We expect people to come alive and *live* out of their heart-to-heart connection with God.

We have fallen into choosing our pastors according to this conviction. To begin planting our last two congregations we asked our cell leaders to identify the people they saw expressing the gifts that go with being a church-planting pastor. Then we got those chosen together under the guidance of our present leaders and they spent months thinking and learning together to sort out who would be the most likely next leader. Our process has not always resulted in the most likely candidate — on paper, at least. We've found that *listening* for how the wind of the Spirit is blowing makes more sense than matching data with job description.

The regeneration inaugurated with the resurrection is bigger than our logic. Through Jesus, the Spirit of God re-ignites our amazing ability to create until we are living in synch with God's Spirit, expressing the deep things of God as they are given to us. Being part of the body of Christ is an opportunity to get a life and express it. We're a community of co-creators re-energized by our connection with God and each other. We're alert to our spiritual center like bees hiving around our queen. I'm happy if we are a wind (of the Spirit) tunnel, where one can't help but pay attention to the fact that God is alive and near.

## Living and Dying

To be born again means that the born-before is as good as dead. To keep accessing life in Christ, we also keep dying in many ways. To succeed at living, also means recognizing how we are failing. As Jesus shows, there will be no resurrection without suffering. We're all about that. We a lot like one of the mutants in Heroes, first season, who ends up passed out on the floor after painting his mysterious pictures that are crucial to saving the world.

A few pages back I was excited about all the babies being born around here. But most of our friends are not there. The vast majority of people our age in Center City, especially, are living alone in a little apartment. Many people over the age of thirty are still not married, much less having babies! The main reason for this, I hear, is not just that they are locked in hook-up culture; it is because they have not succeeded in mastering their place in the economy. Being alone is mostly an economic choice. They don't have the money; they are still in school; they have huge debt; they want economic control of their lives before they make a relationship commitment. As a result they are risk-averse, anxious.

I think they are enslaved. They are scared, at the core, of what they are created to become. Coming to full life, much more bringing another person to life, requires risk. You can't make a baby if you won't risk the connection to conceive. You can't become new if you can't stop perfecting the old.

So we try to give people a lot of chances to exercise their possibilities. We like it when disempowered people get up on *their* shaky milk crates: risking, maybe suffering, possibly failing. For instance, we recently we started asking almost anyone to write for our website blog. It is a little scary to let everyone be our mouthpiece, but it works remarkably well. Similarly, a woman recently took the lead to start another thrift store in our terrible basement on Broad St. The dream could have been an expensive disaster, but it turned out to be remarkably profitable. All sorts of faith, hope and love are always taking big risks to get expressed. Who is to say what is worthy

## EXPRESSING OUR NEW SELVES

of being expressed? We often say that success is showing up. God is showing up, so show up!

I hope we are always a place for the young and other usually-disrespected people to have their dignity, and to receive honor for their natural talents and supernatural gifts. Not long ago we put a nine-year-old up front to lead us on Christmas Eve. There were more-experienced people who would have done a better job but they couldn't have done *her* job. We long for our children to show up, too. We don't want to incarcerate them in programs until they are adults. Like the rest of us, they are who they are, and valuable as they are. We expect them to express the life they have been given.

On the other hand I hope we are always a place where uninspirited things have the right to die. If no one on the sidewalk pays attention to what's happening, does the activity have intrinsic value? If the Spirit of God is not blowing some spark into life, we don't want to hold on to what's burned out. I wish that about 75% of the theological innovation the Catholic Church incorporated between the year 1200 and 1930 had been given the right to die by now. As it is, we keep meeting people whose hearts are hardened from going to *Assumption of Mary* High School, or something. Our brilliant ideas that are no longer much use should have the right to die, too. Once something gets established, it is usually hard for it to be dislodged. But God should not need to come at us like a hurricane.

Not long ago, we considered letting our original Thrift Store die, since it seemed to be on its last legs and we couldn't bear to see it suffer. (We didn't want it to kill *us*, either!) Now it is flourishing. About the same time we began a risky experiment with our congregation in Northwest Philly to see if it had any life left in it. Now the congregation is dispersed. Discerning when something is alive or dead, much more when it is worthy of life-saving heroics or euthanasia, requires a lot of deliberation. We keep deliberating. Just because we observe Lent or have a mission team devoted to urban farming doesn't mean we *need* to! Cells die. Mission teams die. Whole congregations die. I hope we let the whole church die if we no longer risk enough to be truly living and growing.

It is kind of embarrassing but we seem to need to relearn some things all the time: we don't decide where the wind comes from; we can't control much; we no longer need to feel ashamed that we are unable to make everything turn out right. We accepted our need for a Savior. Now we trust God to actually *do* something. And he does.

## The dignity of being alive

We want to be *"born again,"* created and recreated by God. We're serious about the dignity, the responsibility and the opportunity of being truly alive. That is the life we have and the life we express. We are expressers. It is a lofty kind of conviction full of high expectations.

When it comes to God, it seems like many "Christians" settle for a lot less dignity. Does it seem to you that instead of showing up when God shows up, a lot of people want to find an attractive, inexpensive religious gas station? They like to drive up and get some religion pumped in, get a vicarious sensation of someone else's emotion and passion, then roll out with their spiritual motors revved up. It seems like a lot of people are content to get faith delivered like TV — something gets beamed in and happens inside them. No expression is required! No relating is required — don't even need to interact electronically. You can do it in your jammies — don't even need *work* clothes at all! If some people could get Jesus out of a catalogue, they would order him online! (I wish that were outrageous — one of us is considering how to make a circle of hope for the avatars who already live in cyberspace, as we speak.)

People keep going the direction of being locked way up in themselves: inexpressive, unconnectable, living off someone else's passion. I saw it played out again on TV the other day. A "Pentecostal" healer was looking into the camera being very charismatic, revving up our motors. He was about to place his hands on a woman, who was trembling with expectation for whatever was about to happen to her. She was all about getting, with no expectation of expressing.

Something hit her. It felt wonderful. That was apparently the goal, to passively get hit.

I've had great experiences like that. Something turns my switch. I'm over the edge and flying like a flip on a spiritual stunt bike. I think most of us like those experiences, Christian or not. In these numbed-out times in which we have enough money to think we could get what we want and we have seen enough advertising to tell us we'd better get it before it is gone, we have tended to sit around all day hoping something will happen and we will feel it. I probably can't tell you the number of times I have violated the training of the next generation by insisting that they need to show up to relate to God — they are convinced that spiritual experiences are not real unless they just "happen."

I like moments when ecstasy "hits me" too. But that is not enough for us. One of my mentors was fond of saying, "Impression without expression equals depression." Oneness with God, being touched by God, receiving the gift of God, being incorporated in the life of God, always results in becoming one with others, touching others, giving gifts, embracing others with life — or we don't have the life. We would rather let Circle of Hope die, than deprive anyone of their responsibility to keep it alive. God expressing himself in us is all we've got; there isn't anything else to make us who we are.

## "How?" seems to be the inevitable question

Even during his short, nighttime visit with Jesus, Nicodemus was well on the way to learning that he needed to get a life. He was a quick study. He asked the right questions, and didn't mind looking stupid when he asked them. He listened to what he saw, and heard, and felt, and responded to God drawing him back into relationship.

Jesus quickly uncovered why the whole process of relating to God Spirit to spirit was going to be hard for him — like it often is for us. Listen to a bit of his story again.

Nicodemus said:

*"'Rabbi, we know you are a teacher who has come from God.*

*For no one could perform the miraculous signs you are doing if God were not with him.*

*In reply Jesus declared, "I tell you the truth, no one can see the kingdom of God unless he is born again."*

*"How can a man be born when he is old?" Nicodemus asked. "Surely he cannot enter a second time into his mother's womb to be born!'"*

If you are one of the people who can't stand "born agains" let's use a variant way to read what Jesus is saying — "*no one can see the kingdom of God unless they are <u>born from above</u>*" —regenerated, made new, infused with life. The kingdom of God is where God reigns personally. To live there, each of us needs the kind of life that *can* live there — a life that has the spiritual integrity to survive. If we don't receive that life from God we won't even be able to breathe the spiritual air — living in the kingdom would be like landing on Mars and getting off the ship without a space suit. Jesus tells Nicodemus a truth which any spiritually-attuned person could understand. But the learned man doesn't immediately get it. So he asks a variation on the kind of question that keeps him, and many of us, from understanding:

How? *"How can a man be born when he is old? Surely he cannot enter a second time into his mother's womb to be born!"*

We are all born into space and time, so we certainly like to know *how* things work! Our parents have to teach us *how* to eat, after all! No doubt that is why American Christians in the 1800s fell in love with the altar call. You could do a one-time act of devotion and be good to go from then on! — How do you get saved? Go forward and receive Jesus! That's tidy. We like getting things settled because we are, generally, beings who can't consistently remember *how* to get to our car when we get out of a theater! We need help. We need to know how.

The problem comes when we think we have gotten all the help we need. From out of the storehouse of the huge brain we all have, we consider all the connections we have made to survive so far and come to very silly answers to "How?" Then we take our answers and end up questioning God, just like Nicodemus was doing — *"I know how things work, so what do you think you are talking about, Jesus? According to me, it is impossible to be born in any way but the way I was born."*

Nicodemus sounds so silly when I talk about him this way. I suppose when I meet him in the age to come he will chuckle about that time he met with Jesus. He obviously told the story to John and did not bother to make himself look that good! But I am not sure he is any sillier than most of us. We sit down to pray and we ask: "How does this work? Why don't I feel connected to God?" According to the formula we all seem to know, one sits down, asks God for something in faith and it happens, right? It is risky to follow formulas. We often get to: "It didn't work the way I thought it should, so God must be wrong." Our answers to "how?" get in the way all the time.

We operate a main goad to this problem each week. We call it the Public Meeting. The church has always worshiped in public and there are not that many new things a church can do. But we don't need many new things because the things we do cause enough questions to be asked as it is. How can a non-singer express their heart through song? How can a non-relater endure all this groupness? How can an intelligent person listen to a speaker who is not as informed as she is? How can a fearful lover throw himself into communion or prayer? We don't look for conformity in how to practice worship (and that's good, since we have about fifty different worship leaders!), but we do arrange the meeting for people who will express their worship however they can, at whatever level they're on.

## The inevitable discovery is that things don't "work" too well

Receiving the Spirit has a lot to do with waking up to reality without our incessant pragmatism blurring our screen. We always want to know *how* things *work* so we can apply our efforts to things that *work*. We're strangely efficient, as if we did not want to waste ourselves — "There is only so much of me to go around!" We fight about how we think things should work all day; and when something goes wrong, we're upset. When something is likely to go wrong, we're anxious.

Jesus helped Nicodemus get back to being a work of God rather than being like God in his work. Go back to that part you memorized earlier. Jesus told Nicodemus something like this:

*"Your self is a nice creation, but that's not all there is to you. You have a built-in connectivity with God — but you don't live out of it.*

*Here's the evidence of what I am saying. I am God standing face to face with you and you can't even see me for who I am. It's a problem.*

*Feel the wind I am blowing on you with your true self."*

Working with God is something like that. We hope Circle of Hope is a place where we can keep learning to feel the wind of the Spirit in our sails.

In <u>The Gay Science</u>, Frederic Nietzsche wondered out loud if modern people had killed their ability to relate to God altogether. Were you required to read his parable in college? It goes like this:

A madman rushes into a marketplace in broad daylight holding a lighted lantern. He calls out, *"I seek God. I seek God!"*

The people in the marketplace ridicule him, *"Has he got lost?"* says one.

*"Did he lose his way like a child?"*

*"Is he hiding? Or is he afraid of us?"*

The madman turns on them and shouts, *"God is dead, I tell you and we have killed him, you and I...But how did we do this? Who gave us the sponge to wipe away the entire horizon?... What was the holiest and mightiest the world has owned has bled to death under our knives."*

It is not so much that Nietzsche was saying that everyone became an atheist. His aptly-held critique is that the believers had no consciousness of God in their everyday lives. Their lives were not an expression of God. They were practical atheists; they had killed God in the everyday. Isn't that what Nicodemus was doing when God was alive to him in the person of Jesus, face to face? Jesus told him the truth and Nicodemus responded with: *"How can this be?"*

There are many ways to blunt our connectivity. In the U.S. the most common way is to be a good capitalist. Perhaps you have already assessed this chapter according to how much you are "getting out of it." We usually don't do anything that doesn't bring enough profit for our investment. We are much more attuned to the "invisible hand" of the market than we are to the wind of the Spirit. We are moved all over the country by our employment opportunities. But many of us have never made a decision based on a conversation with Jesus. Moving with the "invisible hand" seems practical but moving with the Spirit doesn't.

One of our friends read this chapter and responded like this: "I'm glad I got the Bible content boot camp; it has come in handy. I'm really glad that since then I've learned to sit in silence and just be loved. In my rebellion against the chains of my youth, I've gotten pretty good at the silence thing. I still study, but I really love to sense the movement of the spirit. What was missing most from my teenage training was the expression of all that knowledge. Thinking back on it, I react incredulously, "What was all that FOR? — to win an argument with WHOM?"

## The answers come in the expressing

The way the story is told, it seems like Jesus responded to Nicodemus, "puffed up" with a lot of knowledge, with a little irritation. But I'm not sure that wasn't just the way Nicodemus remembered the moment. Chances are, Jesus spent the whole night with him teaching him "how it can be," and Nicodemus figured out "how it can be," so he could tell the tale to John later from the place where he knew "how it can be."

We did not get broken off from God instantly and our re-grafting doesn't "take" instantly. We have to express the hard, life-and-death questions, even wrong-headed questions, to get rooted and filled. What we should learn from Nicodemus is that God will listen and will help us. We will be going through remarkably hard things again and again — things that shake faith. We'd better be able to talk about them. Just like Daniel Schorr questioned the intelligent design of God on NPR when Katrina leveled the Louisiana and Mississippi shoreline, we will go through hard things that make us ask God some questions:

How can I...
- ...be brought so low in New Orleans?
- ...have cancer?
- ...lose the affection of my child?
- ...have an entire faulty system of belief in my head and heart that works automatically?
- ...be so offended by how much someone in the church has hurt me?
- ...continue to sin addictively?...

...and yet feel the Spirit of God energizing me?

"How can I be born again?" Nicodemus asked.

Jesus said to Him: "You are Israel's teacher, and do you not understand these things?

I tell you the truth, we speak of what we know, and we testify to what we have seen, but still you people do not accept our testimony. I have spoken to you of earthly things and you do not believe; how then will you believe if I speak of heavenly things? No one has ever gone into heaven except the one who came from heaven—the Son of Man. Just as Moses lifted up the snake in the desert, so the Son of Man must be lifted up, that everyone who believes in him may have eternal life."

Until the end of the age, there are going to be lots of questions. The answers come in the expressing the resurrection life that has already been given. Jesus did not just rely on his testimony to reveal the life of God; he expressed it with his whole being. He was lifted up in suffering love and he was the first born from the dead. It is his *living* of the life that brings new life to the world; he's not just talking about it. Likewise, whenever we express such life, we set ourselves on a course toward understanding heavenly things.

Sometimes our artists are the best teachers of life in Christ. They kind of bypass our rational and learned defenses and hit the spots that connect with God. One time during Advent, I think, the team installed a long box filled with sand through which we were to take a "journey." It was a simple, but profound way to meditate. One of my friends, who is a bit OCD, could not stand the idea of letting his feet touch the same sand as everyone else. I encouraged him to wear shoes until he could, but to go on the journey, somehow. The challenge the artists presented helped him consider what he could express and how he goes about doing that.

Of course, the artists have to learn to express themselves as creatures and not Creators. Our cultural worship of "self-expression" has reached its flower in art, so whatever is written or sung or expressed in some medium has a "right" to be. I prefer the anarchy of free expression but I resist the tyranny of tolerance. Our artists are on the cutting edge of understanding how a creature can be wildly themselves in Christ and not deluded by their own creativity. So sometimes what is on the wall is downright perverse. Other times you have to laugh out loud with wonder at how well you just heard the Spirit.

## Respond to the wind

Circle of Hope is not a very good university, and that disappoints some people. They "come to church" like they come to "class" and we say things like, "Spiritual growth is like being a tree planted firmly by living water, but being flexible enough to move with the wind and send out seeds." It just doesn't feel normal. They are experiencing a "paradigm shift." We're not interested in planting a monoculture farm with drip irrigation in the desert; we want to be a big, diverse ecosystem panting with the life of the Spirit. We celebrate that diversity and flexibility in all our public expressions of art and worship and teaching. By the time some people figure out "how it works," something more is working. The next person to arrive is adding to the canvas or someone else has just arrived at the next level of their spiritual development and has further things to offer. We expect those offerings. The one way we admit we are not a "safe place" is when people don't want to take initiative, own their dignity or join in the dance.

I think expressing one's new self can feel pretty scary when you're up on a milk crate or just trying to stand on your own two feet. Like the swimmer about to dive off the blocks into the race, we need to get composed. Take a deep breath:

<u>Inhale</u>. Jesus says this: *"Everyone who believes in me may have eternal life."* We have permission to may live that eternal life. Breathe it in.

I really mean it. Let's pause to breathe it in. Show up. We often take a few minutes to exercise our connectivity with a "breath prayer." It helps us make the word of God to us as near and regular as our breathing. Try using the phrase, "Everyone who belongs to me may have eternal life" to focus on receiving resurrection life right now.

Out of God's eternal life we express our gifts, talents, art, mission and worship. So we need plenty of times and disciplines to receive it. That's why we keep setting apart our Sunday meetings and whole seasons of the year, like Advent, to learn to receive. We go on retreat; we teach each other in our cells, so we can learn to breathe in new life. When I sit down each morning to remember who I am in Christ, it is like I am putting up my sail to catch the wind of the Spirit. It is an art that brings me life.

Then <u>exhale</u>. Jesus acts this way: "We speak of what we know, and we testify to what we have seen." *He expresses it.* Following his example is truly living. We are called to go his way. Let the wind move you.

We are here to live! We are co-creators, Spirit-deliverers, love-builders, eternity-planters. It doesn't matter if what we have seems small, we give it. If you can bake, bake. If you can counsel, do it. Listen? Do it. Lead? Do it. Serve? Do it. Fix someone's bike? Do it. When we honor the Spirit of God in us we cooperate with our rebirth — and with the transformation of the world.

CHAPTER **12**

# Leading as a Team
*The Story: Jesus prays for us, John 17*

There are a lot of different models for how to be a pastor. Some of them come directly from the unbelieving culture, of course: pastor as *CEO*, pastor as *social worker*. I was recently visiting a friend's congregation and it looked like he was pastor as *Holy Spirit*, since he was running around like crazy being the answer to everyone's prayer. It was tiring to look at. Then there was another friend who was pastor as the *voice of God*. He appeared from behind the podium, gave his speech, and then disappeared out the back like some mysterious smoke. Then we had barbeque. When I received a wafer from an Episcopal priest in a robe, it seemed kind of maternal to be fed — pastor as *mother*. There are quite a few options. We're going with pastor as *player-coach* and all our leaders are part of a *team*.

    I never really aspired to be the pastor of the church, and that might be the blessed way to become one. That might be the way God expects his leaders to start out — surprised, resistant and confused. That's how it worked with me (and Moses, among others). During my early college days, when I was still motivated by all that training I received at the feet of Bill Bright and Campus Crusade, I was about as aggressive as I could get about influencing as many people as I could to become followers of Jesus. I influenced all over people! The strange next step was that I became the exuberant and foolish leader of a band of converts. I still remember waking up at some point and realizing, "Oh &%$@! I'm the pastor!" This rude awakening started quite a wrestling match with God. I was not too interested in going there.

My experiences with pastors did not motivate me to become a leader for the church in any way — not if I was supposed to be like one of them! For instance, one of the pastors of my youth horrified my unbelieving parents with his shiny suits and convertible Cadillac — that leader actually had to be restrained from punching the head usher after being accused by him of some fault during a "business meeting" (that same head usher was later arrested for embezzling from the bank)! The pastor I served under during my college years was famous for screaming from the pulpit during his 45-minute sermons — we dutifully attended, but brought paperbacks. I really had no interest in being one of those! So it took a long time for God to convince me that He would show me the way he wanted me to lead and not stuff me into some ill-fitting role.

In that sense, I was blessed and still am. I would just as soon be fired than end up as some "head of state," or figurehead, or any head no one will even talk to anymore because she's the pastor! I keep insisting that the only reason I am into what I do at all is because I *have* to do it to follow God as who I am. I'm not disappointed over what God has given me, but I don't pretend I serve as pastor because it is a peachy job. It is a good life, but I think it is a terrible job. Leadership has its privileges and beauty, but I don't recommend it unless you need to be there. If a person wants to be the leader because they think it will be cool or because they think *they* might be cool if they were the leader, I'm suspicious.

## Did Jesus Aspire to Leadership?

I think Jesus seems like a rather reluctant leader himself. His heart is in it, but the trials and tribulations of leading people around and taking the beating (literally) that the point person takes, seem to

## LEADING AS A TEAM

exasperate him and wear him out. Just a few instances suffice to reinforce that point:
- His leadership does not always come to encouraging results. Jesus walks toward his disciples on the Sea of Galilee and they think he is a ghost; Peter gets out to join him and he sinks. Later on, his right hand man will betray him altogether.
- His leadership is constant, suffering servanthood. Jesus is constantly under attack by the scribes and Pharisees, accused, in one of the funniest scenes in the Bible, of being a liar and possessed. He is persistently denigrated by the political leadership of his nation and is paraded in front of a mob by Pilate, wearing almost nothing but blood.
- His leadership is painful! As his prayer in the garden demonstrates, Jesus feels he has to do what he has been given to do. But it is also clear that he'd rather be doing something else, if he could arrange it.

Jesus is our model.

As usual, Jesus has an upside-down-feeling approach that is rather hard to grasp. Love rules. Rulers love. Listening determines responses. Responders listen. Leaders are servants, servants lead.

The profound prayer in John 17 represents His hope for the leaders he has been grooming and for those who will follow after them, clear down to me. One way to understand how Jesus wants his church to lead and be lead, and the church leaders to lead and be lead, is by listening to him praying for what he wants to see happen among the core team of the first congregation He planted.

John sets up the account of the last night Jesus spends with his followers beautifully. He fills in where Matthew, Mark and Luke have been very factual and brief, expanding on the mysterious meaning behind all the events. As he writes his account, he has to be reflecting on his many years of being a leader himself and pondering how to work out the immensity of what God is bringing about in Jesus. On that final night, the ultimate leader who is going ahead of his followers to prepare their entry into the fullness of re-creation is very concerned that they understand what he is doing. As we look at the heart of what Jesus is working for when he prays, we enter into the heart of his leadership.

## It has been granted to give to all you have given me.

Jesus prays: *You granted [me] authority over all people that [I] might give eternal life to all those you have given [me]. (John 17:2)*

It seems to me that many people, and many Christian leaders, are mostly interested in the kind of *authority* that Jesus has been granted. They think leading is all about having the power, and that is a problem. It is especially a problem for people who have grown up under leaders like Richard Nixon, who was paranoid about his authority, and George Bush, who has exercised his power wantonly. The former dramatically undermined trust in all leaders, and the latter divided the country in dramatic ways, the impact of which remains to be seen. Both claimed to be Christians, with something of a divine right to rule.

Jesus actually did have a divine right to rule, but the language with which he prays about his authority is so humble! He even speaks of his authority being "granted" to him, and being granted so he could grant it to others — to give eternal life to those who have been given. Leadership is all about that grace-filled giving. It is certainly is not about getting stuff for one's ego or pocketbook.

Circle of Hope has about forty-five cell leaders right now and a few of us could not get elected to secretary of the fourth grade, much less President. Some of us hold our power with such fear it jumps out of our hands and conks people on the head. Some of us don't seem to recognize that we have any authority at all. Some of us exercise our authority like mom or dad did — but with less skill. But, of course, some of us are getting downright sagacious!

Even though our bags of skill-levels are decidedly mixed, what makes the network function so well is that our leaders humbly respect that they have been given something to give. For instance, "Don" is so unassuming and deliberate, most people would not think of him as a leader — a person who is supposed to make speeches or who throws grenades while leading the charge. But he gives his time and love and care and people are given a place to be and a place to give what they have been given, too. I think that is good leading.

You can imagine that sharing all that power doesn't always work out real well. We like to say that "people have the right to drive our car," but that means they can wreck it, too! One time a person grabbed the microphone during worship and started giving a "prophecy." People were so used to us being random they thought this was part of the evening's plan. He talked about how one of our leaders was having illicit sex. Most people didn't hear what he said too well, anyway, and the band just played on. But the Leadership Team got more than a little anxious! There is something called too much anarchy! So we got together with the "prophet" and gave him a more orderly way to prophesy. His allegations were checked out with the accused and denied. But you know what? We found out later he was telling the truth! Ultimately, Jesus better be our leader, or we are in deep trouble. He has rescued us from our leaders many times, which gives people confidence to get in the drivers seat. As long as the Giver is respected, what we have been given to give will work for good.

## All I have is yours and all you have is mine

Jesus prays: *Now they know that everything you have given me comes from you. For I gave them the words you gave me and they accepted them. They knew with certainty that I came from you, and they believed that you sent me. I pray for them. I am not praying for the world, but for those you have given me, for they are yours. All I have is yours, and all you have is mine. And glory has come to me through them. (John 17:7-10)*

We started another political season in Philly not long ago. The politicians lined up to succeed John Street, who had been the mayor for most of Circle of Hope's existence. Mayor Street got right to the edge of applying his Seventh-Day Adventist brand of Christianity to his work, especially in his rhetoric. But when it came to sharing, he drew the line. He was a painstaking pie-divider. Dividing the spoils, often influenced by the richest person at the table, is a deeply-ingrained Philly political habit. During the primary campaign, the Mayor's would-be successors jockeyed to get a large enough piece of the Democratic Party pie to win the nomination, which wins the election in this bluest of blue places.

Jesus, meanwhile, is a leader who shares everything. He is eager to share himself. He is bequeathing his world-changing mission to what seems to me like a rag-tag group of doubters! He shares his very life, all his strength. He belongs to others. This way of leading seems odd, at the very least, in a land where private property, human rights and "being all you can be" are idols most people worship. We live in a place where individualism is considered healthy. We are in a "mine vs. yours" world, and Jesus lives in an "ours" world. To lead like Jesus is all about sharing.

We have our own brand of politics as Circle of Hope. I don't think most of us understand it, but we're living it just the same. We're also in a season of change, ourselves, as John Street's sun sinks into the west. We're challenged more than ever to see if we can share. We've set ourselves up as three congregations (and we've had two others that died and are expecting one more, right now) but we are one church. So the pastors and the congregations have to share. We practice an, "*All I have is yours and all you have is mine*" kind of love. It sounds great, and we actually think it is great. But it is hard to share when one congregation makes more money, or one congregation receives more people, or one congregation has more musicians and one congregation has deeper leaders. We don't always take comfort that everything comes from God. Instead, we are tempted to compare how much is coming from us or going from us, and we can quickly produce charts to calculate that in our minds. When the leaders follow Jesus in sharing, that is good, hard leading.

Our pastors are a team. Our cell leaders are a big team lead by a collection of leaders who coordinate smaller teams of them. We leaders often remind ourselves that if *we* can't get along and work together as a team, we are out of business. That was easier when we were 50 people. Now we are over ten times that, it becomes more obvious all the time why the Serbs and Croats could end up killing each other. But we decided early on that either we need to actually reveal the glory of God shared with us by sharing it, or close shop.

## One as we are one: I in them and you in me.

Jesus prays: *I have given them the glory that you gave me, that they may be one as we are one: I in them and you in me. May they be brought to complete unity to let the world know that you sent me and have loved them even as you have loved me. (John 17: 22-23)*

A scandal made a big splash in the country not long ago concerning the leader of a big church in Colorado who had national leadership among evangelicals. He was deposed for using drugs with a male prostitute. For many people, this was just one more ho-hum reason not to trust leaders — which is not an extreme reaction, since most people don't trust them anyway. For others it was a wake-up call about how strangely alone leaders can be. Especially in the church, where a lot of people think leaders need to be perfect, the inability to trust anyone with one's less-than-perfect life causes deep secret-keeping. Some advisors actually counsel a pastor to make sure he or she doesn't *really* trust any friend who lives closer than an hour away! The idea is that they should keep their private life as far from those they lead as they can, because people like the façade of the pastor to be solid — you don't want loose lips to sink your ship (remember Bill Clinton!).

Jesus, coming from an entirely different place, is talking about a unity that is so transparent it reflects the unity he has with the Father! He prays that the way his followers live, love and lead together will allow the world to see God. Our unity in love fills the earth with the knowledge of God. I'm not sure a leader in the church is leading, if they are pretty much doing it alone, or as an image, or as a fountain of fleshless principles. Leading like Christ is about doing it together.

Our relative poverty as the Circle of Hope *forces* us to do things together. For instance, I think the leaders would love to be able to write a check, at times, and let the *contractor* have all the relationships it takes to put together a mission station. But we have to figure out how many people can use a hammer or finish drywall at any given time. We've built togetherness into the heart of how we do things. All our cells begin with a leadership team of Cell Leader, Apprentice and Host. We've proven many times that the more together the team, the livelier the cell.

Sometimes, of course, being thrown together into the middle of a project (like the redemption of the world or rehabbing a building shell) can make us a little *too* transparent. We still laugh at the horrible situations we got into when we were dealing with an inexplicable landlord and unscrupulous contractor in 2005. I actually had a screaming fight in the middle of the street with the contractor who was trying to rip me off again — I call it a moment of rehab "opera." The audience was amused and appalled. I'm still mostly appalled. The fact that the project got done and we did not get as ripped off as bad as we might have been makes the memory of my weirdness a little easier to swallow. I wasn't exactly demonstrating my unity with the Father! But my Father was with me, nonetheless. When we speak of oneness it isn't a uniformity that gives all of us a consistent basket of rights and privileges, and it isn't a demand to respect diversity that protects our personal basket of identity among the whole. Our oneness is relational. It comes from having a common life with God, just like Jesus. We need to lead *our* way in a world where power and identity are defining issues for all sorts of decision making. But we don't need to conform to those assumptions.

## So, as usual, leading like Jesus goes against the grain.

Jesus is a leader. He has drawn disciples into leading with him. At his last supper with them, He prays for a oneness that reflects his desire for them to lead in the same manner he has been leading after he is gone — by giving, sharing and doing it together. He *gives* them the bread and *shares* the cup with them as they eat *together*. That's the setting he chooses to invest with the meaning of his crucifixion and resurrection. We call that the communion meal, since it represents our return to oneness with God. Our leaders lead to catalyze the restoration of that oneness. Communion is where we come from and where we are going.

Such deliberate, visionary, demanding leading flies in the face of the prevailing attitude of people who think they have escaped from following anyone, including Jesus! Being followed as a leader in the mission of the church scares people half to death, they have so many good reasons not to trust any leaders! I feel their pain; I have always kind of felt that way myself! After all the revelations about so many priests of the Catholic Church, and the cover-up by their leaders, many people have gained a particular fear of *church* leaders! Who wants to sign up for that?

What's more, when Jesus insists that leading be done in unity, he confronts the post-modern doubt that it is even possible to trust anyone but oneself, or to do anything but what one can do alone, or to touch anyone but who's in front of you. John Mayer's song, *"Waiting for the World to Change"* kind of sums up the prevailing attitude.

*"Me and all my friends, we're all misunderstood.*

*They say we stand for nothing and there's no way we ever could.*

*Now we see everything that's going wrong with the world and those who lead it*

*We just feel like we don't have the means to rise above and beat it*

*So we keep waiting, waiting on the world to change.*

In an interview, Mayer pointed out that he would not have gotten far if he wrote a song that told people to, "Go change the world." Not only do most people (John Mayer's age, especially!) not respond to being told what to do; they are quite sure they *can't* change the world, certainly not by telling it what to do!! So when Jesus pointedly tells his followers to "Go make disciples and I'll be with you until the end of the world," that sounds a little dissonant in a lot of postmodernish ears.

In my few visits to Christians in other places around the world

(I've mentioned Colombia and South Africa, already) I have come away with a better understanding of some of the reasons Christians in the U.S. don't work too hard at leading. They don't think they *have* to work on it! They are already "sitting on a lead," you might say, content to ride on their power and protect their identity. Some Christians in Colombia, quite differently, risk their lives to lead people out of the morass of corruption and violence that has ruled their country for 40-plus years. Christians in South Africa did a dramatic job of leading their whole nation to prevent a post-apartheid bloodbath and to learn reconciliation. Christians in the United States helped, in the past, to abolish slavery, feed the hungry and create a lot of the social safety net we now take as a matter of "rights." We underestimate what it is really like to have grown up in a place so rich, so defended, that a person can "live off the fat of the land" until they are thirty-years-old or more. There is no need to make too much effort to even preserve oneself, much less lead others to some kind of victory over unbelief, oppression or poverty. In the church, most people were raised to manage programs that "meet felt needs" or to preserve museum-like buildings and liturgy created in a vibrant past. They've never had to do any apostolic work. From lack of leadership, and perhaps the lack of any need for leadership, the church has actually created a new apostolic age in a post-Christian Europe! Many "developing world" Christians already believe that the U.S. is in need of missionaries right now! Many people see post-Christian ways creeping from the cities, primarily East Coast cities, into the heartland.

In our small way, we are leading a way out of all that "whatever." To some, Circle of Hope seems like a very strange place to be so leader-driven, since we're full of people who could easily say, "*Me and all my friends, we're all misunderstood.*" A lot of those misunderstood-type people are in charge around here and are grasping the means to change the world! Granted, sometimes people have had a hard time discerning who the pastor is, and we don't have our Cell Leaders wear special uniforms (although the tattoo threatens to become one in some quadrants), and, as many people have told me, it is no surprise if someone very surprising ends up in front of one of the Public Meetings leading inexplicably. Nevertheless, we press on. We deliberately proliferate Cell Leaders who are pastors of their circles of ten, we call out Mission Team Leaders who lead their teams, and we expect hands-on pastors for 200-person congregations to keep rising up among us. This year we're getting more organized, so we're calling together the Circle of Hope Operations Team to refine the administration of our far-flinging enterprises — it's the CoHOp, deliberately acronymed to sound like co-op. We're trying to be like Jesus, calling together leaders to send them into the complex and demanding task of re-creation.

## We're looking for enablers

When I say "enablers," I'm not talking about the psychological disasters who help you do what you wish you could stop. I'm talking about leaders who care about where you're going and are given to giving a hand. They help you do what's hard to do and try to unleash the best in you.

One woman I know of had a troubling situation moment with her leader and talked to her therapist about whether she should do as her pastor asked. What he wanted her to do was have a session with him after each appointment with her therapist! He needed to find out whether she was getting out of line in therapy! She decided to politely refuse, which was a good moment of personal growth! We don't want to be like her pastor, controlling rather than unleashing.

Leaders entrust, not just command. They give permission to the things that need to be set free, not just keep things predictable. They nurture, not just marshal. They reproduce leaders, not just produce programs, using people as raw material.

## We need enzymes

I know that it is kind of unseemly to compare one's leader to elements of one's digestive system. But in a system as organic as the body of Christ, the enzyme that keeps things moving is really very crucial. Otherwise we are all stopped up in 1730 or 1950 and feeling pretty toxic and looking way full-of-it! The leader comes alongside and catalyzes what God wants to do with what he has given us. Sometimes things take a while to get moving.

Not to push it too far, but the Holy Spirit is even called the one who comes alongside and, like an enzyme, attaches to elements in us to cause a beneficial reaction. One time, one of my mentors preached a sermon with the title, "The Problem with the Church Is the Pastor." (He really did.) Hearty "Amens!" were voiced by all. The problem was that he only changed his mind about himself! His speech was strikingly humble and quite endearing, but he was still in a suit, behind a pulpit, supposedly speaking the word of God. He never managed to come alongside, which might have solved the problem.

We don't want our leaders to sit on a throne and direct people. We think everyone has the Spirit of God and Jesus is, ultimately, leading. The leaders are especially attuned to listen for the Spirit and sense what needs to happen. They are relied upon to catalyze what needs to move with Who moves us.

## We love entrepreneurs

I know enough anarchists to be a little concerned about loving entrepreneurs. I'm not too sure about the shock troops of capitalism, either. But I do love creative people who just want to do something and to make the most of what they've got. When Paul is trying to get to Spain, there is little doubt that he has some kind of franchising scheme in mind. The leader in Christ has an endless ambition born of endless possibilities.

In general, people who come into relationship with our community aren't interested in making something great happen. For one thing, they are probably living in some kind of tiny tribe that takes up most of their energy, so they aren't looking for more responsibility in a larger one. Even more likely, they don't care too much about what happens, or care if anyone is leading things somewhere or not. They don't vote (like most people), and they don't riot, even when there might be a cause. They live off the ample crumbs of the U.S. table and don't worry about producing anything, since the Chinese have that covered.

But once people get next to Jesus, they get the itch to "produce" a changed world. That makes it hard not to lead. Circle of Hope urges people to feel the need to lead, because our church does not produce "church" for attendees to consume (at least very well!). Our Cell Leaders don't organize weekly programs at which members get programmed. We don't provide a booklet to memorize on your own. We provide leaders to be lead and lead.

No one should be forced to lead. If you don't *have* to lead because God is motivating you to make something happen, don't do it. But if you don't want to lead, don't be surprised that the world does not change. You may not want to do it, but that doesn't mean that you couldn't be just as called as Jesus was.

You may have more to offer than you think. You might be just who God needs in a given moment, a particular place, or for a period of time, to let the world know that Jesus was sent and that God loves them even as God has loved you. Once you hold that truth sincerely, you end up making goodness happen. Jesus is praying for each of us, and for our whole team, to take the lead in doing just that.

CHAPTER **13**

# Sharing Resources
*The Story: Jesus and the Seventy, Luke 10*

For half of Circle of Hope's existence, the whole country has needed a neck collar — at least! Just when we were about to recover from our whiplash, another disaster rammed our bumper. September 11 and the subsequent wars in Afghanistan and Iraq put a lot of us in emotional traction. Then we had a whole year of hurricanes which put New Orleans in perpetual ICU. Those were just a few of the major jolts.

In general, people were pained, spiritually laid-up, overwhelmed, numb *before* there was a smoking hole in New York, a sodden hole in New Orleans and a festering hole in Iraq. And the jolt of adrenaline that came with each new emergency did not keep them conscious for long — it is just too daunting to stay awake! Being numb can seem so practical, especially when the society encourages it! I don't think most of us think it is *right* to just pull the covers over our heads, but it is hard to peek out when our society pushes every enhancement to our avoidance mechanisms known to humankind — from inebriates to mood enhancers, from yoga to soap operas, from multi-billion dollar gambling towns to Three-million-square-feet malls, to *Return of the Mummy* ad nauseum. Everything pushes us toward sedation.

It is hard not to avoid reality when all around us there seems to be an underlying sense of suspicion that, "Bad things are about to happen," or "Something is about to explode, and I'd better keep out of the line of fire." If one is philosophical, she might fear that our godless experiment in individualism is about to bear some final, horrible fruit. If he's economics-minded he might fear that we have taken as much stuff as the rest of the world will allow, and now they are going to charge the border of the "homeland" to get some back, or at least deny more pillage to our armies overseas. Or maybe you don't need to think big at all to find something to avoid. In my neighborhood we regularly witness the free exercise of the very-protected right of impoverished teenagers to procure hand guns. Fortunately, the neighbor who tried to nab Jane's purse after a Shalom House meeting didn't pull one out!

Even though one might expect her to be well into sedation, my 80-year-old mother usually calls me after the latest bad news to inquire of her most religious of sons, "Do you think this is the end?" (And she is not talking about this book!)

I usually ask her, "Are you ready for it to be the end?" She already has slow-moving cancer and has lost a husband, so she is all about mortality.

She says, "I think I am. But I don't like the way things are!" She proceeds to tell me how things should be. Even in her weakened state, with plenty of reasons to live in blissful denial and with plenty of skills to perfect some numbness, she can't help caring about what is going to happen. Maybe all she has to share is her outraged opinion, but she gives it.

## It is amazing how much people share!

When things get scary a lot of people get numb. But an amazing number of people share. Life can hand us massive difficulties, but in the face of that, a significant amount of our neighbors keep offering mass quantities of goodness! People often wonder out loud how any God could allow the world to get so bad. But when you look at it another way, you have to wonder how so much good can be happening in such a terrible place! We're quite a creation! It is amazing how much people are willing to offer! — rich or poor.

In the rubble of the world or in the breakdown of a life, I am always amazed to find hope waiting to connect with hope. If I smile at a downtrodden-looking person at the dollar store, a brilliant smile is likely to break out. If I pursue a numbed out person long enough, they often recover their strength to believe. Jesus helps us to remember what we've got to give and moves us to share what we have for the hope of redemption and love.

Here's an example of some of that innate need to share that Jesus regenerates and uncorks. After September 11 the stories about hope meeting hope just kept on coming. Here is a story of someone with some resources to share as excerpted from *Marie Claire*.

*A 24-year-old woman just had to do something after the attack. Her 30-year-old brother was a firefighter for one of the first squads to respond to the World Trade Center. When her family learned her brother was missing, she cried all day but then just couldn't sit still anymore. So she headed for the makeshift volunteer center located a few miles north of the disaster site. The scene was chaotic. Masses of people were lining up to board buses headed down to ground zero to help with search-and-rescue efforts. She fantasized about finding her brother, half-conscious, reaching out to her from underneath the rubble. After sunset, many of the waiting volunteers got tired and went home. She stayed and helped lug boxes of blankets, flashlights, and fresh clothes onto trucks for the site workers. At around 11 p.m., a group loaded onto a bus to go to ground zero, and she sneaked on with them. As they rode downtown, people lined the street on both sides, waving, holding signs of encouragement, even handing us food through the windows. They yelled, "Thank you! You're heroes! We love you!"*

*When the bus full of volunteers finally reached the site everyone fell silent. The scale of the devastation was so huge, it was impossible to take it all in. But there was no time for tears. They had work o do.*

*She raced to grab a hard hat and shovel, and quickly joined the* ranks of hundreds of others shoveling. She filled bucket after bucket with soot, metal, computer fragments, office memos; sometimes using her hands. Every so often, workers would pass by carrying a body bag. But she didn't break down—partly because she was still in shock, and partly because she had to stay focused on the critical nature of the mission. There was a feeling of calm on the scene as everyone quietly worked, hoping to find survivors. But then, thunder and lightning began. When a hard rain started falling, the rescue was suspended.

She never found her brother. But she did not regret her time spent at the scene. She sees it as a tribute to her firefighter brother, who gave his own life trying to save others.

When we were first talking about this story, remembering rubble while new rubble was being produced in Iraq, it helped me understand how God looked over his creation and said it was good. Of course he looked at the terrorists who killed 3000 and he looked at some government officials who neglected the poor, and at some who sent potential disaster prevention money to execute a trumped-up war in Iraq and said, "My creation needs to be redeemed!" But people keep showing why it is so worth redeeming! The kind of sharing that erupts when people are in need is incredible. We know this personally, since lots of people helped us when they heard there was a Circle of Hope in Philadelphia rehabbing demolished people and rubbley buildings! It is that kind of incredible sharing that God keeps using to redeem us.

## Jesus unleashes the power of sharing

One way people say you just *have* to end up believing that we are created beings is that you can see the creator in us. When you see us sharing, you have to wonder, "Where did all that sharing come from?" I have a problem believing that it is a matter of the luck or logic of evolution that produces the goodness that keeps sprouting up. Regardless, sharing exists, and people who connect with God learn to perfect it. They are freed to demonstrate a touchable, selfless love like God reveals in his own Son, as he shares his life.

We're working at getting more and more unleashed to demonstrate that God-like love. Our convictions as Circle of Hope include this thought about sharing like God shares. We say: *"sharing our resources brings freedom and unleashes power."* At my Coordinating Group meeting one day a young mother quickly said, "I couldn't even think about being at this meeting or leading a cell if I didn't have our community helping me care for my children." We like feeling the freedom and power of sharing.

But we don't share merely because it feels good. We *have* to share or we can't follow Jesus — at least not practically. Most of us aren't rich enough to hire all the people it takes to run a nuclear family or to buy one of the hugely-expensive row homes in the neighborhood. Much less could a handful of us have the money to carve out a meeting place for the church or sustain a pastor or care for the needs of the poor all around us. If we don't share our time, money and love there is no way our church could survive in this town, much less provide for our mission. One of our secret strengths as a people is that a lot of us put our money where our mouths are. We don't just *talk* about community; we *are* a community that includes our money and other resources.

We keep learning the fullness of what is built into us as Jesus rebuilds us and sends us out with the freedom and power to share his life, just like God shares life in Him. It is that basic. The incarnation is about sharing! It is no surprise that lessons about sharing were among the first lessons Jesus taught "the seventy" as he sent his disciples out to represent him on the very first missionary journey.

## How Jesus sent out the seventy, and us

Americans tend to be overly concerned with "what works." And we think of "resources" as money, time, or energy — as material or physical things. But great methods with lots of stuff behind them don't change the world enough. Jesus sent the disciples out on their first mission with a lot more than what they could carry. Money and property are good tools, but they don't pay the spiritual bills! The essential resources Jesus offers to those who live in the rubble the world keeps creating, or to those who are lost in the flood that keeps lapping at levees that never hold back the water, derive from the very heart of God.

When Jesus sends out followers, he uses their time, their energy and, maybe some of the money they've been trusted to carry. But he doesn't send us out to *merely* give people time, money or energy or anything else that they thought would "work" and didn't. He sends us out to give people resurrection life. The ultimate resource Jesus is sharing through his followers is the reality that the kingdom of God is near. The Lord sends out his disciples to prepare the way for God to share himself in the person of Jesus. They are the presence of the coming kingdom of God.

Luke 10:1-20 contains a fascinating look at how Jesus sees what he and his followers are all about. We often think of sharing in purely material terms. But this is how Jesus considers material things when he is sending out his people:

*Do not take a purse or bag or sandals. Stay in that house [of a person of peace], eating and drinking whatever they give you.*

Isn't He saying, "Being a beggar will be fine?" Isn't He saying, "Don't bother taking anything, the material things will follow the spiritual things?" If we are preoccupied with, *How?* and *What?* or *Where's mine?* and *What's theirs?* people will just stay stuck in the usual rut and won't get what they really need. People need God near more than they need anything else. So we need to try not to cover God up with a lot of stuff.

Being poor or in need of stuff is not irrelevant, of course, like some Christians seem to think. I agree that, "If you want peace, work for justice." The enforced poverty of others creates judgment on whole nations! So we are sure to voice our conviction about sharing stuff. But we don't just talk. For one thing, we try to create a Common Fund that is truly common, because lack of sharing material resources strangles the heart of a church and makes whatever we might say a joke. Even more, like I said before, we keep nurturing a whole non-profit corporation (Circle Venture) to keep goading us into sharing what we have and creating an alternative community, because we want to erode the place of evil powers that oppress and impoverish.

But just sharing our money or stuff is not the whole answer to what people need (albeit, a minimally-tried one in many places). The fact is, Jesus has bread to eat that people don't know about. He sends his disciples out to share it. He told them, and tells us, *"Do not even rejoice when the spirits are subject to you, but rejoice that your names are written in heaven!"* Meaning, among other things, "Don't take pleasure in being able to manipulate the physical realm. The life of the Spirit is going to invest the physical with much more than you could ever squeeze out of it without God."

## So how do we share?

There's that "How?" word, again. Jesus needs a filled heart to use, not a "how to" book to be followed. But that doesn't mean he doesn't have a lot to teach us about what to do. He uses six pictures in Luke 10 to describe how we are to share this new life God is sending into the world. It is a good way to end the book, since by now it is evident that there is a lot we have to give!

1. <u>Go as farmers</u>. He told them, "The harvest is plentiful, but the workers are few. Ask the Lord of the harvest, therefore, to send out workers into his harvest field."

*"Go into your harvest fields Circle of Hope and friends."* We have a few "farmhouses," in South Philly, Fishtown and Camden, a couple of supply sheds on Woodland Ave. and Wayne Ave. Everywhere a cell meets is a place where a field is getting irrigated and planted. Our tribes of friends, our workmates and our extended families and friendship circles are full of unplowed spiritual frontiers.

Essential to being a worker is planting verbal seeds and reaping the response to the good news. Tell them the kingdom of God is near; Jesus has come and died and risen. The Spirit of God is unleashed in the world and new, eternal life is springing up. We have the keys to silos full of seed, you might say — *"Whoever receives you, receives me,"* Jesus says.

2. <u>Go as lambs</u>. Jesus told them, "Go! I am sending you out like lambs among wolves."

The lambs have the resource of their utter dependence on God to share. Just like Jesus is the Lamb of God who triumphs over sin and death, we don't use wolf ways to get to lamb ends. *"Go out among the wolves Circle of Hope and friends*, get out of your pen and depend on me. They can't kill you."

We've proven the power of being dependent repeatedly. It is so "lambish" to think giving away CFLs or bottling Unda Water will change the world — after all, don't the wolves own the world? We lambs of God don't think so. We create cells full of marginally-functional people and expect God to transform them; and God does! We set up a counseling center that lets Christians be therapists and God untangles people and sets them free. Our weakness is our strength.

3. <u>Go as peacemakers</u>. Jesus was training them to share, "When you enter a house, first say, `Peace to this house.' If a man of peace is there, your peace will rest on him; if not, it will return to you."

The peace of God is more than peace on earth. It is not just lack of injustice or lack of war; it is rest in the middle of suffering and chaos. It is being safe in God when the world is not safe. *"Go Circle of Hope and friends, bring that peace to people."* Teach them; insist on it. If they tell you their war-making is peace, your peace will return to you. If they trust in the Prince of Peace, your peace will remain.

The kingdom of God is upside down compared to what passes for "normal." Wandering around looking for partners in peacemaking seems counterintuitive to people trained to search out and destroy threats to security. Nevertheless we have bought a house for Shalom House at 51st and Pine because we found some people who want to share their passion for peace in the middle of the world's largest war-making machine. They recently took in an Iraqi refugee.

4. <u>Go as guests</u>. Jesus taught them the humility to receive care, to even call out care by being as needy as we are. "When you enter a

town and are welcomed, eat what is set before you."

Just like Jesus came to Matthew's house and to my heart and sat down to dinner, receiving what he was served, that is how we go. We say that "Jesus is best revealed incarnationally" — person to person, by loving within another person's context, by being empathetic, by understanding, through acceptance, and by being humble. Jesus is less concerned with "my way of life" and "my comfort" and "my people" and more interested in lovingly entering the life and appreciating the place of another.

*"Circle of Hope and friends, keep entering new territories with grace."* South Philly Italians, children of immigrant Jews and underground artists are your landlords. Asian, African and Hispanic immigrants are your neighbors. The youth of the nation are moving into your city. Long-time, so-called black and white neighborhoods are blocks away. Eat what is set before you with love. Share the resource of your grace.

5. <u>Go as messengers with signs</u>. As they announced that the kingdom was coming to town, the disciples were to expect miraculous signs to validate their message. Jesus said, "Heal the sick who are there and tell them, `The kingdom of God is near you.'"

God keeps filling up a storehouse in each of us and among us. It is not just filled with logic, personality or wealth (although those are all good, too!); it is filled with His Spirit. As we go, God comes with us; and as we share, God comes with our stuff. God has been there before us; Jesus is coming after us. The sign of God's presence is that people are healed — maybe in their body, often in their minds and hearts, surely spiritually. Our resource is God himself, with us; the kingdom is near.

We know we are fighting the sin addiction, so change is rarely instant. It is exciting when it is instant, and we have seen plenty of quick miracles. But most people need the demonstration that God will be near them through the long process of their recovery. We are here to stay. Just recently a person who had been considering following Jesus for years among us was finally baptized. Likewise a person who had been addicted for years finally gave up the cocaine and met Jesus in rehab. Our ongoing presence and perseverance in faith is one of the biggest signs of all. *"Go, Circle of Hope and friends, and keep going. Relentlessly pour health into the sickness around you."*

6. <u>Go as prophets</u>. Jesus told them to say to people who would not receive their message: "Even the dust of your town that sticks to our feet we wipe off against you. Yet be sure of this: The kingdom of God is near."

*"Go Circle of Hope and friends and tell the truth."* Discernment and fearless, gracious speech are resources that are so sorely lacking in our society it hurts! We need to keep telling the truth to the powers that be: "Government, don't tell the poor people of New Orleans that it was their own fault they died." And we need to be kind but bold to individuals: "Jesus is the Lord of all, not just another religious figure to loop into your god-concoction." People need us to deliver their spiritual nerve transplants! So many are like people who can't feel heat, so they keep sticking their lives into the flames.

The first thing Jesus told his disciples when he sent them out amounted to, "Don't worry if you think you have nothing. I am with you." We rely on that, since we don't have a lot of money or all the other resources we would like to have.

People can do a lot with nothing. We're an amazing species. After Hurricane Katrina, stories poured out of New Orleans about how devastated people helped each other and how people went around the ineptitude of the government to get involved. That's still happening. Here's a story about someone with no resources to share, one of the "looters" we heard about from the newspapers, in this case, excerpted from the *Cornwall Times*.

*Jabbar Gibson, who was reported by an American television channel to be just 15, was determined to leave New Orleans after two days wading alone through the filthy waters of the former red-light district of Storyville. Although he had never driven a bus in his life, he broke into a school and made off with the bright yellow vehicle. "I knew how to get over the fence, and where the keys were, so I felt it was worth the chance," said Gibson, whose age was given by another channel as 18.*

*Although he had only eight passengers on board when he set off on Highway 10 towards Texas, Gibson picked up many more, young and old, stranded beside the road during the eight-hour journey. "By the time we got to Houston we had all kinds of folk on board, from mothers with young babies to people in their seventies and eighties. And when we ran out of gas we had a whip-round and everyone gave me enough cents to fill up.*

*The young driver, who was still looking for some of his friends and family, said he was not worried about the legal repercussions of driving without a license. "I don't care if I get blame for it so long as I saved my people," he said. "If we had stayed there, we would still have been waiting."*

People have a lot of resources to share built in, even at Ground Zero or in the middle of the Lower Ninth Ward. We are an amazing creation. Jesus comes to reclaim his rightful place as Lord of creation and to redeem the broken beauty of it. He sends us out with his message: "The kingdom is near." That is the resource upholding all the other resources that we share. The astounding reality into which we are invited is our utter dependence on God and His utter dependability. Hope meets hope. We can trust God to be near. And God is near, insisting that we share his life like he shared it with us. And we will.